LIVING
— by —
CHOICE

LIVING
— by —
CHOICE

*Making the Decisions
That Define Your Life*

MICHAEL L. NELSON

GOOD CHOICE PUBLICATIONS, LLC

Published by: Good Choice Publications, LLC

Special editing by: Christina Roth
Cover and book design: Longfeather Book Design

Paperback ISBN 978-0-9996589-0-1
Ebook ISBN: 978-0-9996589-1-8

LCCN: 2018900312

Dedication

In memory of my grandparents,
Rush and Lucille Morton,
who taught me about life with love, kindness, and
a genuine caring about other people.

Contents

Living by Choice
Who Should Read This Book

Adults Wanting to Make Better Choices

All of us need to brush up on our choice-making skills from time to time. *Living by Choice* will help adults reflect on the importance of their choices and possibly identify choices they need to make to develop a more meaningful and enjoyable life. No matter our age, new choices can add new interests, new opportunities, and new dimensions to our lives. As the book stresses, it's never too late to make a good choice.

Parents Teaching Children

Living by Choice can serve as an excellent guide for parents who want to teach effective choice-making skills to their children. Each of the choice topics can be used to create an educational session in which parents explain and discuss a specific choice with their children. Such sessions can help children understand the importance of their choices, gain a better idea of what to do when they face one of these choices, and understand how important their choices are in defining their lives. Collectively, these topics provide a choice-making course that will help children develop the understanding that "you are who you choose to be."

Young People (12 to 21)

Young people today are growing up under the influence of external information available 24/7 via the phone in their hands. Such information includes no-holds-barred comments and videos on social media and other types of websites. Every day they are exposed to texts, tweets, photos, and messages that can influence them, often in negative ways. *Living by Choice* is intended to help young people recognize the importance of: 1) being an independent thinker; 2) treating other people in kind and respectful ways; and 3) making more effective choices as they work to define their lives.

An Opening Thought
The Power of a Choice

You seldom get what you go after
unless you know in advance what you want.
Indecision has often given advantage to the other fellow
because he did his thinking beforehand.

Maurice Switzer, *Letters of a Self-Made Failure*

We're so busy with our daily routines—including school, work, and family activities—that we seldom stop to think about what is required to manage our lives effectively. We tend to live our lives one day at a time without an overall strategy for how best to do so. We can live our entire lives without ever gaining an understanding of how our choices define who we are and ultimately what we achieve.

To bring this subject into greater focus, I have written this book to help you consider the choices you are making in your life. I'm certainly not saying you will find "the answers" here, and that was never the intention of this book. In fact, the ultimate answers about your life can only come from you. I would, however, like to stimulate your thinking. My objective, therefore, is to help you think about your life and motivate you to make any choices needed to adjust the way you are living yours.

As the quote above implies, those of us who know what we want to achieve enjoy a decided advantage over those who do not. Meaningful goals are important to have. But without the willingness to make the choices required to turn those goals into reality, they're just something nice to talk about.

Therefore, it's the choices we make in support of our goals that are important. Our choices not only determine if we will achieve our goals, but they also determine the type of person we turn out to be. John C. Maxwell, author of *Beyond Talent*, highlighted the importance of our choices this way:

Life is a matter of choices,
and every choice you make makes you.

With good choices and the willingness to see them through, you and I can accomplish almost anything. The eighty-two topics addressed in the following pages will help you think about many of the choices that are important in life. Each will take only a few minutes to read, but I hope you will ponder them even longer. If you would like to make personal notes as you read along, space has been provided at the end of each of the fourteen sections.

I confess, there is some repetition within the book ... many life-defining thoughts are worth repeating. And some of us need to read things more than once for it to sink in. Therefore, there are some basic points you will encounter multiple times as you read the book. As examples, three of the most important ones are:

We are here for each other.

You and I are not here to live our lives just for ourselves, but to help others have better lives as well. If there is a secret to living a meaningful and fulfilling life, it's remaining mindful of the needs of others and helping others in your own special way.

Our life has a built-in purpose.

If we are attentive to our interests, our motivations, and the needs of others, our purpose will at some point become clear to us. You and I are here for a reason ... to do something special with our lives. It's up to each of us to determine what that is.

There is some goodness in almost everyone.

No matter our past, we still have an opportunity to increase the goodness our life produces through the future choices we make. It may include showing concern for friends and neighbors, reaching out to help improve our community, or devoting our life to a work or cause that would make the world a better place.

But we have to remain mindful of how powerful our choices can be in shaping our lives and impacting others. As examples, concerning the three points I've just outlined, you have choices:

> You can *make the choice* to help other people in your own special way, or choose to be generally unconcerned about those around you.

You can *make the choice* to work to discover what you were brought into this world to do, or choose to forget about the intended purpose of your life.

You can *make the choice* to be kind and respectful toward others, or choose to ignore the opportunities you have to expand the goodness within you.

Take a few seconds to think about how powerful your choices really are. You can use them to accomplish good, meaningful, even great things with your life. *Or* they can be used to create difficulties, hurt other people, and be the reasons you miss the opportunity to do something special with your life. No question, our choices define the individuals we are today, and who we will ultimately be in the future.

Managing the power of choice,
with all its creative and spiritual implications,
is the essence of the human experience.
Choice is the process of creation itself.

Caroline Myss, *Anatomy of the Spirit*

Making and managing choices … that's what life is all about.

An Opening Question
Where Will Your Choices Take You?

The Opening Thought reminded us how powerful our choices really are. They, and the work we do to implement them, are the primary factors that determine what we will achieve with our lives. Our choices can take our lives almost any place we want to go. So, this begs the question … where will your choices take you?

Your choices can take your life many places …

Through your choices, you are, in effect, telling your life what you want it to do … where you want it to go. Some of these places might include living an honest life, being respectful of others, apologizing when such is required, letting love guide your life, setting high expectations and valuing what's inside of you. These and other "choice places" are addressed in more detail in this book.

… but your life also has a message for you.

Your life is also speaking to you … trying to tell you and guide you to what it wants to do. Some of us are good at math, for others it's language. Some want to be outside, others indoors. Some are excellent speakers, others prefer to write or paint. Some are interested in biology, others in technology or the environment. These preferences are really clues your life is providing to you … leading you to what is referred to in this book as *the intended purpose* of your life. So, another question … how do you determine the intended purpose of your life?

Determining your life's intended purpose.

Ultimately, this is a decision—a choice—that only you can make. People can offer help and assistance, as we are doing in this book, but no one can make this decision for you. It's one of the most important choices you will ever face, but there is no set way to make it. However, there seem to be three basic groups of clues that, if you pay attention and think carefully about them, will help you make this determination. These include:

Personal Interests (*brain-driven*). These clues start to show up at a very early age and are some of the first indications of what you are intended to do with your life.

Internal Motivations (*heart-driven*). There are feelings that you have ... maybe they make total sense, maybe they don't. But you feel them pulling your life in a certain direction.

The Needs of Others (*people-driven*). Because we are here for each other, your life's purpose will become clearer when you consider how you will use it to help someone else.

The challenge is to determine what, collectively, these clues are saying to you.

The mystery of human existence lies not in just staying alive, but in finding something to live for.

Fyodor Dostoyevsky, The Brothers Karamazov

But it still depends on the choices you make.

Utilizing these clues, you may achieve a "clear sighting" of your intended purpose in life, but never come close to achieving it if you aren't willing to follow where it leads. That's why our choices are so important ... our life can lead us to our basic purpose, but, because we make other choices, we turn around and head off in a totally different direction.

So, where will your choices take you? Regardless of your past experiences or your circumstances today, your choices and the efforts you make to implement them will be the most important factors in determining what you will achieve with your life from this day forward. Therefore, it just makes good sense to work to become the best choice-maker you can possibly be.

LIVING
by
CHOICE

1
MANAGING YOUR LIFE

Each of us is charged with the responsibility of managing our life. While we may receive assistance during our early years from parents, teachers, and friends, at some point we become the primary decision maker and the choices about our lives are left to us. The outcomes of our life management work include the type of person we turn out to be, the extent to which we use our life to help others, and what we ultimately accomplish with the life we have been given.

CHOICES ADDRESSED IN THIS SECTION

The Choice to

Be the Leader of Your Life
Be an Independent Thinker
Be a Talker or a Doer
Accept Responsibility
Be the Difference
Establish a Business Plan for Your Life
Finish What Your Start
Do It Today!
Make the Effort
Beat the Odds

The Choice to
Be the Leader of Your Life

Whether it's a country, a company, or an athletic team, the success of a group's efforts is highly dependent on its leader. Effective leaders help us establish important and worthwhile goals, motivate us to work together to achieve them, and cultivate a sense of responsibility for actual results. In spite of any challenges or difficulties that may arise along the way, groups with good leaders work to produce meaningful results. On the other hand, groups with poor leaders tend to wander along, conduct themselves in selfish ways, and, in the end, accomplish very little.

We talk frequently about leaders in government and business. However, we seldom stop to think about the fact that each of us is, in effect, the leader of our life. We exercise this leadership through the choices we make. If our life achieves worthwhile things, it's because we have exercised effective life leadership. Ray Kroc, who built McDonald's into the most successful food operation in the world, gave us this insight about self-leadership:

The quality of a leader is reflected in the standards they set for themselves.

Sometimes, we simply abdicate our life-leader role. We blame our poor performance on other things. We're not smart enough, not pretty enough, not lucky enough, or have "issues" that hold us back. But that's not what effective leaders do. Instead they guide us through tough times and difficult situations. Your life is no different. Your choices guide you to better things, or to worse.

What are the most important qualities of an effective life leader?

First, you have to be honest.
People can spot a liar—or truth stretcher—from miles away. In addition, whether it's your subconscious ears or your brain

subliminally at work, your life knows when you are not being honest with yourself or with others. Honesty helps you deal with all things—good and bad—and productive life leaders recognize the importance of being honest in everything they do.

Second, you have to conduct yourself in a proper way.

You have to show others, and yourself, that you really do believe in doing things the right way. How you live your life day-to-day speaks to you as well as those around you. Effective life leaders set important life goals and show a desire to accomplish something that is beneficial for everyone, not just for themselves.

Third, you must be willing to commit to achieving more.

Productive life leaders want to improve, to achieve things, and to make progress regardless of current circumstances. People rally around an important call to action. Your life is no different. You put your life in gear when you commit to achieving something important to you and those around you.

Effective life leadership inspires us to dream more, learn more, do more, and become more. We not only improve ourselves when we exercise such leadership; we also become an example for others to follow. Thomas J. Watson, the former chairman of IBM, explained the relationship this way:

> Nothing so conclusively proves a man's ability to lead others as what he does from day to day to lead himself.

Leading ourselves to be more and do more is a responsibility that has been given to each of us. It's not a responsibility we asked for, but one that comes automatically with our lives. The effectiveness of that leadership is almost totally dependent on the choices we make. You and I must think carefully and work diligently to become effective life leaders. We have been given a life. It is up to us to prove that we can lead and manage it in a special way.

The Choice to
Be an Independent Thinker

We place a high value on being accepted by others. Accordingly, we can be influenced, in some instances even controlled, by what those around us are saying or doing. If we don't stop to consider why we're doing something and what influences are affecting us, we can go to great lengths—even make some poor choices—just to become more acceptable to others.

The problem with allowing our lives to be overly influenced by others is that we assume they know what they're doing. Or that what they are suggesting will work for us. In reality, this is just not the case. Not only can we be misled by friends and others, but, while that's happening, we can miss the opportunity to define our own lives and become the unique individuals we were born to be. You can be the leader of your life or you can let others lead you. This is a choice that each of us has to make.

> *The individual has always had to struggle to keep from being overwhelmed by the tribe. But no price is too high to pay for the privilege of owning yourself.*
>
> Friedrich Nietzsche, German Philosopher

As you work to be more independent and decide things for yourself, keep these points in mind:

What's on the inside is more important than what's on the outside.
To achieve the life we are intended to have, we must listen to the signals coming from our hearts and minds to guide the choices we make as we establish the direction for our lives. We must maintain our independence if we are to read these internal signals correctly. We must, therefore, be willing to turn away from others and make our own decisions, especially when we are being influenced in some improper way.

It's a risky choice to automatically accept what others are saying or doing.

The process of becoming an independent thinker starts by coaching yourself not to automatically accept what others are saying or doing. Granted, we can learn things from others. However, it is our responsibility to determine for ourselves if the information and suggestions coming our way are helpful. If you will take your time and think, you can determine when these influences will benefit you and when they will not.

Information on the internet can help you and hurt you.

Cultivating independence in today's world is becoming increasingly difficult as hundreds of social media posts, tweets, and messages find their way to our devices each day. We are encouraged these days to find out what's trending so we can be in touch with the crowd and what they are thinking. We are being conditioned to be group thinkers, not independent ones. Be aware of your online experiences, spend your time there wisely, and don't let others control your thoughts … and your life.

You are here for a reason.

Other people don't know what you are feeling inside, your desires, or what your unique interests are calling you to become or to achieve. When you are overly influenced by the opinions of others, you risk making choices that are inconsistent with who you are, and you can easily miss the opportunity to discover what your life is telling you to do. You are here for a reason. It's up to you—not others—to determine what it is.

Don't miss the opportunity to be the unique individual you are meant to be. Don't pass up the opportunity to do the things that only you feel the motivation to do. Be willing to reject what is popular and be the leader of your life. You life has an intended purpose, unique to you. Don't let others keep you from achieving it.

Your time here is limited,
so don't waste it living someone else's life.

Steve Jobs, Founder of Apple

The Choice to
Be a Talker or a Doer

A talker or a doer ... which are you? As you think about your answer, here are two familiar sayings that might help in your reflections:

Talk is cheap.

This is a saying we've heard many times. Basically, it means that it's easy to say something ... that simply offering our words typically doesn't require much of us. No major effort is required on our part to make an off-hand comment or offer our opinion about something. We tend to think that we have done something significant when we express our view of things. While some "opinionated insights" may have value, we should remember that words alone are much less effective in improving a situation than actually going and doing something about it.

Actions speak louder than words.

We all know that's right. But as we live in a world increasingly filled with texts, tweets, and other bits of information, *doing* something can easily get squeezed out by the words and messages that occupy much of our typical day. We exchange a lot of information, some of it very helpful, but ultimately it's what we *do* that counts. If we aren't mindful of our choices, we can talk our way through life and miss the opportunity—and the significance—of *doing* something meaningful and worthwhile for ourselves and for others.

No question, our words can be important. But our actions play a much greater role in who we are and how effective we are in our daily living. It's one thing to say to a sick neighbor, "I hope you get to feeling better." It's something altogether different to cook the evening meal for her family and take it over to her house. One is just a positive comment lasting a few seconds, but the other requires planning, cooking, organizing, and delivering the food ... conveying a real and tangible benefit. Just saying, "Our city needs to do more for the homeless!" is one thing. But actually volunteering to serve plates at the food kitchen or working to raise more funds for the homeless shelter is so much more. There's a big, big difference between *saying* and *doing*. Confucius, the Chinese teacher and philosopher, made this distinction concerning which is the superior of the two:

A superior man is modest in his speech,
but exceeds in his actions.

Let's be honest here … most of us spend far more time *saying* what should be done than in actually going and doing it. But *doing* is fundamentally important to what we achieve with our lives. Whether it's in our business, family, or community, there are so many things you and I can *do* to make things better. And our *doing* takes on even greater importance when it helps an individual who needs assistance in some way. Helping another person have a better life is one of the greatest opportunities we have for *doing* something meaningful with our own lives.

In performing some research for this book, I was especially touched one day by a large photo of a poor man, dressed in very ragged clothes, who had stopped his bicycle, gotten off, removed his flip-flops, and was giving them to a needy little girl who had no shoes. Wow! If we could all do things like that!

So, spend some time thinking about how often you are satisfied with just *saying* something nice versus actually *doing* something nice for others. As you do, ask yourself these questions:

What can I *do* to help someone in some special way?
What can I *do* to make someone feel that I care about them?
What can I *do* to improve someone's life?

A talker or a doer? Which will you choose to be?

The Choice to
Accept Responsibility

"I don't know why I did that!"

That's a little white lie we pull out now and then to avoid confronting the reason we made a poor choice. There is always a reason behind a decision we make, but frequently we'd prefer not to discuss it. Instead, we try to avoid thinking about our mistakes with a defensive comment like this.

Why do we have this tendency to duck the responsibility for undesirable outcomes? Why do we react like it wasn't us who created the difficulty in the first place? Why do we offer excuses instead of owning up to our mistakes? There are many reasons, I'm sure, but here are three of the primary ones:

We don't want to damage our self-image.

Each of us has a self-image, and we don't want it tarnished in any way. We're afraid that if others think we were wrong or made a mistake, this self-image would suffer. So we protect it by fudging the truth. We do this in spite of the fact that honesty is the most important ingredient in building a strong self-image. It's the act of honesty—not the circumstances of our mistake—that makes us feel better about ourselves, improves our self-image, and enhances the opinion others have of us. Thomas Szasz, the psychiatrist and author of *Personal Conduct* and *The Second Sin*, explained our self-creativity this way:

> People often say that this person or that person has
> not yet found himself. But the self is not something one finds;
> it is something one creates.

We don't accept that our choices define who we are.

We make the mistake of thinking *this one choice* won't have any long-term impact if we just ignore it. We devalue a single choice and think it won't matter much in the grand scheme of things. Well, that's faulty thinking. Every choice we make affects our character—the person we are inside—in some way. Positive choices add to our character, and poor ones detract from it. So being personally responsible for every choice you make—the big ones, the little ones, and those in between—is important because they collectively define the person you are. British historian Arnold Toynbee gave us this view of how our choices define us:

> *My own view of history is that human beings do have genuine freedom to make choices. Our destiny is not predetermined for us; we determine it for ourselves.*

We don't understand how personal responsibility can improve our lives.

One of the most important factors in making a sound choice in the first place is to accept responsibility for the results. If we are willing to charge ourselves with the responsibility for the outcome when we make a choice, the odds of that choice producing positive results are significantly increased. We perform much better when we put ourselves on the line. Cecil Baxter, author of *Later in Life I Learned*, characterized the importance of personal responsibility this way:

> *He didn't get promoted, blamed it on his luck.*
> *But the office gossip was, "he likes to pass the buck."*

So stand up and be responsible for your actions, your words, and your beliefs. Not only will you become a better and stronger person, but others will respect the honest way in which you live your life. No one is perfect, and we all make mistakes. Don't expect otherwise, but do be quick to say to yourself and to others when something goes wrong, "That was my mistake." We can learn from our mistakes and become a better person, but we have to own up to them to do so. Put yourself squarely on the line for the results of the choices you make. Own up to the good ones and the bad ones as well. Accepting responsibility for all of your choices is fundamental to learning how to develop a better life.

The Choice to
Be the Difference

Many of us look around our towns and neighborhoods and identify problems that need to be fixed, but do little or nothing about them. Maybe a park needs to be cleaned up. Maybe the animal shelter needs volunteers. Maybe a special project within the school needs someone to lead it. There are dozens of such situations in every community, circumstances where the need is known, where the potential benefit would be significant, but no one is doing anything about it.

It may be understandable why such situations exist. Funds are limited, politicians have other priorities, and we have our own personal problems to worry about. All of these reasons may be valid and, to some degree, justify the lack of action. But it doesn't have to remain that way. If just one person is motivated to do something and willing to work at it, they can improve almost any situation. It may take time. It may not be easy. It may have the odds stacked against it, but it can be done. Many of us are aware of important needs. But to actually make improvements, someone has to be willing to *do* something as well. Leo Rosten, author of *Religions in America*, explained life this way:

> The purpose of life is not to be happy but to MATTER,
> to be productive, to be useful, to have it make
> some difference that you have lived at all.

Matt White, 30, was shopping in a Memphis grocery store when he encountered Chauncy Black, 16, who offered to "take out your groceries if you will buy me some donuts." Matt, after finding out that the nice young man needed much more than donuts, said, "Come on, I'll take you shopping." Matt helped Chauncy fill up a grocery cart and, after paying, delivered the young man and the groceries to Chauncy's house. When they went in to put things away, Matt found an empty refrigerator, a very sparsely furnished apartment, and Chauncy's 61-year-old mother who had adopted Chauncy and could barely support them with her disability check. When Matt got home, he wrote about the situation on his Facebook page, and the offers to *help came pouring in. Subsequently, he set up a Go Fund Me page that over a period of a few months raised over $300,000 for Chauncy and his mom. Matt was then able to buy them a small house, provide for living expenses, and set up a college fund for Chauncy. When someone asked him about Matt, Chauncy said, "Nobody ever cared the way he did." Matt White-one individual who made the choice to help and changed lives in a wonderful way.*

You can be the difference.

Many times we say that someone can *make* a difference, but in many instances, you can *be* the difference. You can be the starting point in getting a community problem or individual need within your community addressed and resolved. Your interest, your choice, your voice, your work can be the difference in making life better for others.

People will follow.

The idea that something needs to be done to improve a situation is almost always supported. Getting others involved is where things come up short. But when people see that you are taking action, that you are in fact starting to work on the problem, many will join in to help you make it happen. We need individuals—like Matt—to set things in motion. You can *be* the one to do so.

Your choice today can have long-term benefits.

Although problems may start out small, they can grow and become serious situations impacting hundreds, possibly thousands of lives. The fact that you start to work now to improve circumstances could head off even bigger problems in the future and make life much better for people for years to come.

So what will you do when is there a need, an issue, or a problem in your community that comes to your attention? We know that talking will not fix anything. It takes an individual who will stand up, heed the call they are feeling inside, and go to work to make life better for people around them.

To *be* the difference … what a great choice to make.

The Choice to
Establish a Business Plan for Your Life

Many of us prefer spontaneity. Instead of planning, we wait and decide things when and if they present themselves. Some of us don't want to establish important goals because we would have to work exceptionally hard to achieve them. Plus, we would only be disappointed if we fell short. In other words, it's much easier to take life one day at a time, and that's exactly what many of us do.

The problem with taking the day-by-day approach to life is that we seldom accomplish much by using it. We either reach a point in our life when, looking back, we suddenly realize we've wasted a lot of time. Or worse, without a plan to base things on we make some unproductive choices that we now can't go back and change. Flying by the seat of our pants almost never works out well in life. It's more effective to develop plans about how we will live our life … plans that we can use to guide the choices we make.

Managing your life, to a great extent, is like managing a business. In this case, you're the CEO and Chief Choice Maker. Most successful businesses develop well-thought-out plans that explain where they want to take the business in the years ahead and how they plan to get there. Such plans require time and effort to develop and need updates as real-world circumstances or new market conditions emerge. Most of us have goals, but without a plan to achieve them, goals alone are not very effective.

Antoine de Saint-Exupéry, the French author and pioneering aviator, reminded us of the importance of having a plan:

A goal without a plan is just a wish.

The act of writing down our life plans helps us to sort out our thinking. Putting them in writing requires more thought and more detail. Writing these plans down helps us to clarify important goals that we have. And planning helps us create a strategy for achieving them.

What should a typical business plan for our lives cover? Such plans will, of course, vary greatly from person to person and depend on such things as our interests, our goals, and how we would prefer to live our life. The actual content of your plan is up to you. But as you consider what will be in your life plan, here is a list of questions you may want to address and answer in it:

- How do I want to treat other people as I go through life?
- How will I help someone else have a better life?
- What do I consider my most compelling personal interests to be?
- What natural skills and abilities do I possess?
- What do I believe the intended purpose of my life to be?
- Career-wise, what do I want to accomplish with my life?
- Family-wise, what do I want to achieve?
- Health-wise, what do I need to do to take care of my physical self?
- How will I make important choices when I face them?
- How effective are my communication skills and how can I improve them?
- How effective are my writing skills and what can I do to improve them?
- What are my most important goals in life?
- What knowledge or skills do I need to help me achieve my goals?

There are many other important questions you might want to answer in your plan. As you develop these, remember the ultimate question to answer is this: What do I want to accomplish with my life? At some point, you will run out of time and no longer be here, but the consequences and memories of your life will remain. Make sure you know what you want those memories to be, and that you are developing a plan for your life—and making the choices—that will help you accomplish exactly that.

The Choice to
Finish What You Start

One of the things about choices—particularly the difficult ones—is that it's much easier to make the choice than it is to actually do it. *For sure, I'm going to lose this extra weight and get in shape again. Yes, I'm going to start that business that I've been thinking about for years. No question, I'm going to get involved and start volunteering at the retirement home.* The idea of a positive choice is almost always appealing, but actually doing it seems to be a different matter.

As the old saying goes, "The road to hell is paved with good intentions." We all want a better life; we want to do more and accomplish more. But are we willing to move beyond our intentions to turn our choices into reality? The website Statistics Brain, used by over 3 million people each month, indicates that only about eight percent of us actually complete the New Year's resolutions we make. The fact is, we need more *doers* and fewer *talkers*.

Why do we say one thing and intend to do it, but never get it done? There are millions of reasons, but the most common has to do with the amount of work involved. In other words, something was a lot tougher to do than we had expected, and we weren't willing to work hard enough to make it happen. Our brain was okay with the idea, but we couldn't get our body in gear to go along. Author Amit Kalantri explained the relationship between the choice and the work this way.

Beginning in itself has no value;
it is an end which makes beginning meaningful.

Important choices require exceptional efforts. And you never know exactly how things are going to work out when you take that all-important first step. There will always be challenges and surprises. But we learn by doing. One of the fundamental qualities of successful businesspeople—in addition to having a strong work ethic—is the ability to change and adjust to market circumstances.

It should be the same with you and me. We must be willing not only to work at it, but also to make lifestyle adjustments if we want to lose that weight, finish that degree, or successfully achieve an important goal. Michael Jordan, one of the best NBA players of all time, pushes us to keep at it with these words:

If you're trying to achieve, there will be roadblocks. I've had them; everybody has had them. But obstacles don't have to stop you. If you run into a wall, don't turn around and give up. Figure out how to climb it, go through it, or work around it.

We all have things we've been intending to do, or that we started at one time, but never finished. But looking back and feeling bad about it doesn't do much for us. Instead, pull out your list of unfulfilled intentions and select one thing on it that you really want or need to do. Give it some fresh thought, reformulate your goal, and establish a timeline to get it done. Then, make the choice to get started and commit to getting it accomplished regardless of the difficulties or history involved. There's no real secret here. Accomplishing something really important with your life takes a strong commitment and long hours to get it done. Theodore Roosevelt, the 26th and youngest president of the United States, gives us this perspective about life and hard work:

Nothing in this world is worth having or worth doing without effort, pain, and difficulty. I have never in my life envied a human being who led an easy life; I have envied a great many people who led difficult lives and led them well.

Occasionally we start things that do not merit finishing. Circumstances change and our original goal may turn out to be undesirable or unfeasible. When this happens, we must have the courage to stop and reassess things. We may conclude that a wiser course of action is needed. In other words, a new choice needs to be made. The better our original choice, the less likely this is to happen. But when it does, it takes a special kind of wisdom to know what to do.

The Choice to
Do It Today!

Procrastination is like a credit card;
It's a lot of fun until you get the bill.

Christopher Parker, English Actor

The artist Pablo Picasso warned us about the real problem with procrastination when he said, "Only put off until tomorrow what you are willing to die having left undone." Yes, but we are busy people and time flies, as they say, so we just don't get around to doing many of the things we have been intending to do. The problem with such a mindset is that our life is flying by as well. And, before we know it, we run out of time, and our intentions are never realized.

To prevent such a "flyby" in our lives, we should take the time periodically to think about the way we are living. We should reflect on the positive things we have accomplished in the past week. And then, we should go a step further and identify the things we have been intending to do for some time, those things still on our list ... or still sitting in the back of our minds. We should start today to focus on those things we have been intending to do and begin making the choices required to start checking them off the list.

> If you need to be nicer to other people, you can put a smile on your face and start treating them in a friendlier manner ... *in the next few minutes.*

> If you need to exercise and improve your physical condition, you can start walking, running, or going to the gym ... *this afternoon.*

> If you need to lose weight and lessen your chances for certain medical problems, you can be more selective about what you eat ... *at your very next meal.*

If you need to be a more supportive spouse, you can identify one thing that you should do to make things better, do it, and check it off the intended list ... *today.*

If you need to reach out and apologize to someone for something you said or the way you conducted yourself, your phone is there beside you ... *you can call them right now.*

There are other examples we could have included here, but you get the point. The key is to identify the items on your intending-to-do list and get started working on as many as possible. This is where your choices enter the picture again. If you can't make a specific choice to get started on something right away, the odds are it will never happen. That's why weekly think-about-life sessions are so important. They are really choice-making sessions that provide a time to develop your activity list for the coming week and include some of the important things you have been intending to do.

> *My mother always told me I wouldn't amount to anything because I procrastinate. I said, "Just wait."*
>
> Judy Tenuta, Comedian

Most of us have important things that we have been intending to do for quite some time. Although our intentions are good, we haven't gotten around to actually doing these yet. We have our reasons: It's a tough thing to do, we don't really have the time right now, or "I'm going to do it, I just don't know exactly when." If we continue to accept such explanations, we'll never get any of these done.

So check the balance on your procrastination bill. If it's excessive, maybe it's time to make a payment. Maybe it's time to identify the items on there that you need to do and make the actual choices to get them done. Not next week, not tomorrow, but today ... in fact, you can start right now.

The Choice to
Make the Effort

We can make good choices, but fall short of our goal if we aren't willing to make the effort our circumstances require. We can choose to do a lot of wonderful things, but not accomplish any of them if our efforts are halfhearted. We can think great thoughts, but never accomplish great things if we aren't willing to work to make them a reality. Our choices set things in motion, but without hard work, little is ever accomplished. The Greek writer Euripides characterized it this way:

> *With slight efforts, how could one obtain great results?*
> *It is foolish even to desire it.*

Have you ever wondered why some people achieve so much and others very little? We typically think of such reasons as brains, luck, money, or just being in the right place at the right time. Granted, these things can contribute to a person's success, but there is a more fundamental reason that determines what we accomplish with our lives. Few of us get all the breaks, have all the money we need, or are smart beyond belief. However, individuals who are successful find a way to overcome these and other shortcomings. They do it through effort … by working harder and longer to achieve positive results.

It's important to recognize that more is required of us than just making the right choice. We must be willing to do what it takes to turn that choice into reality. The easy part is setting the goal. The tough parts are overcoming the obstacles that keep us from fulfilling the choices we make in support of achieving it. Confucius, the Chinese philosopher, reminded us of the importance of continuing our efforts in spite of setbacks along the way:

> *Our greatest glory is not in never falling,*
> *but in rising every time we fall.*

These words remind us not to let the regret or memory of some bad choices we made in the past keep us from "setting a new course" and making the extra effort to achieve something special and important now. We all make mistakes. The important thing is that we learn from them and use them to provide us with more motivation to work harder this time.

One additional point to think about here is the relationship between the importance of the goal and hard work. You need a worthwhile and challenging goal to fully engage yourself in the effort. Things that are easy to do or don't mean very much to us seldom get our juices flowing. But assigning yourself to a significant goal—something you want badly to achieve—provides a level of motivation and a will to work like no other. Therefore, don't hold back from setting a bold objective and taking on a major challenge in your life even when the work to achieve it scares you to some degree. Fear can work to our advantage, especially when the quality of our life is at stake.

And what could be more significant than establishing objectives that will make your life meaningful and worthwhile? What could be more challenging than finding the intended purpose for your life and working to fulfill it? What could be more important than finding ways to use your life to help others have better and more enjoyable lives? This is difficult work. But only those who are willing to make an exceptional effort are likely to achieve exceptional results.

If you want to develop a special life, the journey will not be easy. But when challenges and difficulties arise, successful people work even harder to find a way to make it happen! You will have setbacks and even moments of defeat in your life. But combining good choices with extra efforts will help you overcome them. Your life has a purpose; finding and fulfilling it is not easy but well-worth the extra effort that is required.

All the so-called "secrets of success"
will not work
unless you do.

Unknown

The Choice to
Beat the Odds

Truth be told, most of us have plenty of reasons why we shouldn't be successful in life. We don't have enough money. We need more education. The jobs available are all minimum wage. Our friends are poor examples. Our family didn't teach us the social skills we need. And on we go. If all we want to do is justify our lack of performance, we can point to plenty of reasons why we haven't achieved as much as we wanted with our lives. But one of the biggest mistakes we can make in life is to just accept our circumstances as "reasons" for our lack of accomplishment.

So what can we do if we find ourselves feeling victimized by some version of these circumstances? What can we do if we feel that the odds are stacked against us? The first thing is to understand and acknowledge that everyone—yes, everyone—has something that they have to overcome to accomplish their goals in life. A successful life is never automatically given to anyone. It is always a project that requires careful thought and diligent work to achieve. Michelangelo, arguably the most talented sculptor of all time, explained it this way:

*If people knew how hard I had to work to gain my mastery,
it would not seem so wonderful at all.*

So, what should we keep in mind as we work to beat the odds we may face?

Your life is a unique package with a built-in message just for you.
Beyond understanding that we all have challenging circumstances at times and that hard work is the key to overcoming them, you should remind yourself that your life contains certain indications concerning what you should do with it. As hard as it may be to wrap your mind around the idea, your life has an intended purpose.

Your interests, your motivations, and the needs of others will reveal that purpose to you if you work to interpret what they are saying to you. The clues are inside of you. And understanding your purpose in life will provide you with an expanded desire and an increased will to work to achieve it.

> *Nothing splendid has ever been achieved*
> *except by those who dared believe that something*
> *inside them was superior to circumstance.*
>
> Bruce Barton, American Congressman

Your choices will take you there.

You can overcome almost any circumstance and achieve your purpose if you are willing to make the choices, some likely to be very difficult, to get you there. As pointed out in the introduction, our choices are very powerful tools that we can use to accomplish important things with our lives. Achieving your purpose—and overcoming the odds against you—will require a series of choices over a period of time. It is through the actual implementation of these choices that you achieve something significant with your life.

> *Destiny is no matter of chance. It is a matter of choice.*
> *It is not a thing to be waited for; it is a thing to be achieved.*
>
> William Jennings Bryan, United States Secretary of State

You can't be lazy if you want to move beyond challenging circumstances. You have to think carefully and listen to what your life is saying to you. The idea is not to live only in the moment, but to become mentally tuned in to what you want to accomplish with your life. As you start to visualize your future and focus on it, you can start making the choices that will turn the motivations and objectives you have today into a purposeful and meaning life in the future.

No question, you can beat the odds if you choose to do so. Many have done it … and so can you.

Section 1
Managing Your Life

PERSONAL NOTES AND REMINDERS

The
choices
we make today
will define our lives
tomorrow.

2

BEING AN
HONEST PERSON

Honesty is the foundation of life. It's the personal quality that influences almost everything we say and do. It's the most important factor in making choices that are correct and right for us. Honesty creates an environment in which we can live in an authentic way. Honesty brings forth the "truth within us" that is so necessary for us to interact in realistic ways with family, friends, and others.

There are no guarantees concerning how effective our lives will be. But the daily adherence to honest thoughts, words, and deeds significantly increases the chances that our lives will be meaningful and fulfilling for us and for others as well. Without honesty, developing a special life is difficult, most likely impossible, to achieve.

CHOICES ADDRESSED IN THIS SECTION

The Choice to

Live an Honest Life
Be Yourself
Value the Person You Are
Understand It All Starts with Honesty

The Choice to
Live an Honest Life

There are two areas of honesty: being honest with *others* and being honest with *ourselves*. The former is subject to public facts and circumstances that can be used to verify what we do and say. In other words, people can usually determine if we are telling the truth or not. The latter, however, is strictly confidential—just between God and you, so to speak. Being honest with others is relatively easy to achieve; being honest with ourselves is often much more difficult.

If you want to tune up the level of honesty in your life, the first thing you should understand is there are no degrees or shades of honesty. There is no such thing as saying or doing something that is "partly honest." You are either honest about something, in what you say or do, or you're not. As John F. Dodge, the automobile manufacturing pioneer, clarified for us:

> *There is no twilight zone in honesty.*
> *Something is either right or it's wrong.*

When telling a story to our friends, we sometimes have the tendency to throw in a few things to make the tale a little more exciting or a bit more humorous. To diminish the importance of such actions we've come to refer to them as "little white lies." But straying from the truth, even in small ways, is a poor choice. When it becomes apparent to others that we're not being honest, we lose credibility and people wonder if they can trust us about anything. Little lies are small steps in the wrong direction, and trust with others, once damaged, is difficult to rebuild.

Being honest with others.

If you want to understand how the benefit of being honest works, it's important to recognize the distinction between the *act* of honesty and the *information* being shared. It's communicating in a totally honest way—not the actual information exchanged—that builds trust between people. It's not the details involved that builds trust, but rather you sharing those details in a truthful and honest way. As Frank Lloyd Wright, the famous architect, explained:

The truth is more important than the facts.

Being honest with ourselves.

This is more difficult because we live under the influence of other people's opinions and want to be accepted by them. As a result, we often make choices based on what others think without listening to what our head and our heart are telling us to do. Without the ability and the willingness to be totally honest with ourselves, our lives are subject to heading off in the wrong direction. The success of many of the choices we make is almost totally dependent on being honest with ourselves—how to improve ourselves, our basic beliefs, and what we want to achieve with our lives, to mention a few. Success in life depends on our ability to be in touch with ourselves. As Ralph Waldo Emerson wrote in *Greatness*:

None of us will ever accomplish anything excellent or commanding except when he listens to the whisper which is heard by him alone.

So being honest with *others* and being honest with *ourselves* are fundamental to living a meaningful life. Each "side" of honesty supports a series of choices and must be well-managed throughout our lifetime. There will be times when you will be motivated to look the other way or stretch the truth beyond your comfort zone … beyond the edge of honesty. But don't do it. Remain true to yourself and to others and be completely honest every day of your life.

If you choose to be honest in everything you say and do, at some point you will look back over your life and be unbelievably grateful that you lived it in an honest way.

The Choice to Be Yourself

Given the influence of social media, the push for us to conform and think like the group thinks has never been greater. There is almost constant pressure, especially on the younger ones among us, to live our lives like others—to wear the "right" clothes, go to the "right" places, and think the "right" things. Because we want the approval of others, we frequently adjust our life in response to these influences in an effort to gain acceptance. However, if we constantly yield to what others think, we can completely miss the opportunity to be the individuals we were intended to be. Raymond Hull, author of *How to Get What You Want*, warned us of the problem of trying to be like others with these words:

> *He who trims himself to suit everyone*
> *will soon whittle himself away.*

Because we don't see or feel such influences changing us, we don't often stop to think how "outside information" is shaping our lives. Nevertheless, it's some of the more important thinking we can do. If we are ever going to develop the ability to make good choices—choices that are correct and right for us—we have to maintain a certain amount of independence and cultivate the ability to think for ourselves. They don't sell pills that help us stand on our own two feet, but that is exactly what we should be working to achieve. Readily accepting the opinions of others will almost always take us in the wrong direction. Steve Jobs again urged us to "do our own thing" with this instruction:

> *Don't let the noise of others' opinions drown out your own inner*
> *voice. Have the courage to follow your heart and intuition.*

We place such a high value on the opinions of others that it is very difficult to free ourselves from them. Because of that, I decided to be rather blunt in making the following points to have a better chance of motivating you to stop and think about these circumstances—more specifically, to choose to reduce the amount of influence others have on your life. Here they are:

Most people don't know what they're talking about.
It's amazing how much credit we will give a friend of ours, while allocating little or no credit to ourselves. The truth is, other people don't know what's going on inside of you, what your life is all about, or what you want to achieve with it. It's a big mistake to listen to people who don't really know you and let them influence you in the wrong way.

As long as you are being good, kind, and productive, it doesn't matter what others think.
No question, you have to be a good person, be kind to others, and work to achieve your purpose in life. But beyond these basics, it really doesn't matter what other people think. So cultivate the habit of gauging yourself by these three qualities, not by the opinions or ideas of others.

You've got your own drummer inside, and others have no way to hear the beat.
You have personal interests, special motivations inside you, and feelings about the needs of others that are leading you to your intended purpose in life. Other people can't hear the "drumbeat" that you can hear and have almost no way to factor your uniqueness into any suggestions they are trying to make.

Granted, there are people in our lives who want to help us—moms, dads, brothers, sisters, teachers, associates, and close friends. These people care about us and want the best for us. But again, as long as we are good, kind, and productive—those three important things—how we live our lives is ultimately up to us and the choices we make. We welcome the love and counsel those close to us can provide, but at some point, you and I have to "drive the bus."

Don't try to make your life look like others. You are unique and special. Believe it and live that way.

The Choice to
Value the Person You Are

We all have some physical characteristic we don't like. For some, it might be their body ... *I need a few more muscles and a lot less weight.* For some, it could be the way they think they look ... *I wish I were prettier and more attractive.* And for others it might be their height ... *I never liked being short and have always wanted to be taller.* Those of us who have such concerns consider them to be real, and, if we allow them, they can be a handicap in living a successful life.

Feelings like these develop when we let ourselves be defined by our looks. Our looks get an undeserved priority because they're what we see in the mirror every morning and what our friends and family comment on from time to time. I'm not saying the way we look doesn't have some importance: slobs tend to impress people much less than those who are appropriately dressed. I am, however, saying that our looks have little to do with who we are and what we accomplish with our lives.

The factors that determine who we really are, and ultimately our success in life, can't be seen. They can only be experienced. And, while our "look" factors can be improved slightly, we can make significant, even monumental, changes to our "who-I-really-am" factors based on the choices we make. We don't have much control over the way we look, but we have a significant amount control over the type of person we are. Here are some of the factors that are really important in life:

How we treat others.

When we show respect and kindness toward others, including people we know and ones we don't, we create an environment that allows other people to feel special, information to be easily exchanged, and friendships and connections to develop and grow.

What we learn and the understanding we develop.

We start life knowing very little, but the more we treat life as a learning experience, the more informed and interesting we become, and the more likely we are to accomplish something special. What you know is a huge part of who you are.

The way we let love guide us.

Love can guide you in very special ways: to people you care greatly about, to concerns for those who are less fortunate than you, and even to the intended purpose of your life. Following the guidance of love can help you become "who you really are."

How hard we work.

Few of us have everything laid out for us. Almost all of us have challenges, obstacles, and difficulties as we try to make life work. How you address these and how hard you are willing to work to overcome them says almost everything about who you really are.

What we actually accomplish.

Excuses, even if valid, don't count very much. What you actually accomplish with your life, in spite of difficulties, is the ultimate definition of who you are. I'm not talking about achieving fame and fortune, but rather using your life to help people in special ways. Erich Fromm, the German philosopher and author of *Man for Himself*, defined the "work at life" objective this way:

> Man's main task is to give birth to himself,
> to become what he potentially is.

Through the choices we make, we have the opportunity to define who we are today and who we become tomorrow. To do this in an exceptional way, we must place a low value on how we look. And place a high value on helping others, becoming more knowledgeable, letting love guide us, working hard, and finding and following our intended purpose in life. But be mindful that people are pushing against you; they want you to conform and be like them. It's up to you and me to keep our lives on our own track and ultimately become the person we are meant to be.

The Choice to
Understand it All Starts
with Honesty

The basics in football are considered to be blocking and tackling. In basketball it's dribbling and shooting, and in golf it's driving, chipping, and putting. In every sport there are fundamental skills and competencies that are considered necessary to play well and to excel in some way. In fact, most great athletes practice the basics as they work to improve their performance. Without executing the basics well, individuals and teams aren't likely to experience much success.

Well, living life has some basics too. The better we understand these basics, the more effective we are likely to be in our pursuit of developing a happy and meaningful life. While we don't consider life to be a sport, there is a strong parallel between how well a great athlete executes the basics and how well we execute the basics of life.

All of these basics are important in life, but the first is far above the rest:

Being honest.
First, we must be skilled at living in an honest way. We must not only be honest in our interactions with others, but we must also be honest with ourselves as we make the choices that shape and define our lives. Without the will to be honest and live in an honest way, nothing else matters.

Helping others.
Aside from being honest, helping others is a major part of what life is about, so it's a definite selection for this list. Your skill in focusing on others and making someone's life better and more enjoyable is a major factor in making your own life better and more enjoyable as well.

Valuing a healthy lifestyle.
The ability to live a healthy lifestyle is a diminishing skill, as more of us are overweight and fewer exercise. However, we must be

skillful in making effective choices about what we eat, how often we exercise, and what we do to keep our "house" in good working order.

Gaining knowledge.

The more we know, the better our skill in making informed choices and the more interesting we become. Such knowledge may come from academics, from our experience in our life's work, or from a genuine motivation to read, research, and learn about something of interest to us.

Confirming our purpose.

The skill you develop in interpreting what your interests, your motivations, and the needs of others are saying to you—and thereby confirming the intended purpose of your life—will place you in a position to maximize the impact of your life, for yourself and for others.

These five basic skills are needed to live life in an exceptional way. Developing your life in each of these areas will require that you make some very important choices and work exceptionally hard— just like exceptional athletes do—to gain proficiency in each.

Billy Williams was a special guy and seemed to be "hitting on all cylinders" as he entered his senior year in high school. He was good looking and well-built. He was a super athlete and had a good chance of leading the football team to a state championship this year. He made excellent grades and likely to finish near the top of his class. But, for some reason, Billy always seemed to stretch the truth. He told several girls he had been contacted by a Hollywood agent, but that had never happened. He told his buddies he had an offer to play football at the university, but it had not been received. He told his teacher that he had an academic scholarship offer from Stanford, but that was not a reality. Funny thing, those around him picked up on his less-than-honest ways, and their view of him had diminished over time. One day, as he walked down the hall, another student said to his friend, "Billy may have a lot of things going for him, but being an honest guy isn't one of them."

A special life requires several things, but, above all else, honest words and actions. Being less than honest overshadows the good qualities we have. Your most important choice: to live an honest life.

Section 2
Being an Honest Person

PERSONAL NOTES AND REMINDERS

*The
choices
we make today
will define our lives
tomorrow.*

3
CREATING
A CARING YOU

When we get up each morning, it's difficult to think about anyone other than ourselves. We have important things to do, problems we have to get resolved, and bills we need to pay. These and other priorities make it difficult for us to focus on anything other than our own circumstances and our own personal needs. But to make life work well we have to create space in our lives for others, to show that we truly care about them, and to use our lives to help people in need in some significant way. Developing a meaningful life doesn't depend on caring just about ourselves. It depends on caring about others too.

CHOICES ADDRESSED IN THIS SECTION

The Choice to

Consider Your Life's Impact on Others
Focus on the Inside Instead of the Outside
Activate the Goodness in Your Life
Forgive
Label Less and Love More
Get Involved

The Choice to
Consider Your
Life's Impact on Others

Our choices have ripple effects, spreading out and touching the lives of those around us. When a young person chooses to study hard and make good grades, the ripple effects are proud parents and the admiration of family members and friends. Alternatively, when someone chooses to be loud and impolite, devoting more time to sarcasm than showing a sincere interest in others, the ripple effects are people who really don't care to be around a person like that. We develop and live our lives, not alone in our rooms, but in conjunction with the lives of others.

So while our personal choices are important to us, we should look beyond ourselves and consider the impact our choices have on other people. Which brings us to one of the more important questions in this book: *Are you living your life primarily for yourself, or are you living it to help others?* Far too many of us are approaching life and our daily routines almost exclusively focused on ourselves. However, the real satisfactions in life come not from living in this self-centered way, but in being mindful that we are here to help others as well.

Acknowledging the real impact that your life is having on others is not easy or routine. We tend to think of ourselves as "a good guy" and don't see a real need to stop to think about how our life is impacting those around us. As a result, we don't actually see ourselves as others see us.

But if you perform a quick assessment of your interactions with others over the past few years, your life will answer the question above for you. If you have encountered more than your share of problems or conflicts with those around you, it's apparent that you are living your life for yourself. On the other hand, if people tend to pull you in and show that they want to be with you, it's almost a certainty that you are showing you care about them. In other words, how you make the other person feel determines their view of you. Maya Angelou, the acclaimed author and activist, explained it this way:

> *People will forget what you said,*
> *people will forget what you did,*
> *but people will never forget*
> *how you made them feel.*

So, are you approaching life and other people in a sincerely helpful and caring way? Or are you more of a self-centered person focused primarily on what's important to you? To make life work well, you should focus less on yourself and your wants and more on the needs and happiness of others. You should almost forget about yourself and work to help others have a better life. If there is a secret to living a successful life, it must be showing more concern for others than we show for ourselves. Les Brown, the well-known author and speaker, outlined the benefit of living this way:

> *Help others achieve their dreams*
> *and you will achieve yours.*

You should note that focusing on the needs of others is not a natural or easy choice to make. We are preconditioned to look out for ourselves. But you can look out for yourself with part of your life and for others with part as well. It's when we leave out the part about caring for others that our life gets off track, doesn't seem to work well, and doesn't bring us a real sense of satisfaction.

Your life touches many people each day. Whether the impact of those touches is positive and good depends on the degree to which you help others and make them feel you care about them. Kindness is very powerful as it creates special feelings in others about you. If you choose to make other people's lives better, even in small ways, your life will be better as well. That's just the way life works. There's really no question about it.

CREATING A CARING YOU

The Choice to
Focus on the Inside
Instead of the Outside

When you stop and think about it, we are really two people in one. The world sees our *outside* while much of our living and who we really are takes place on the *inside*. In effect, we have an exterior life that others encounter and an interior life where we stop and think, love someone dearly, feel concern for someone in need, learn important things, and make life-defining choices. It's easy to see which of these two is the most important ... in fact, it's no contest. But in spite of the importance of our inside life, many of us focus almost entirely on the outside one.

Why do we spend so much time focused on our outside? The answer is simple: we want to be accepted by others. We want others to approve of us and to think we are okay or even special in some way. As a result, we select clothes that reflect what others around us are wearing. We want the latest cell phone or the snazzy car so others will think better of us. We'll even mark our bodies with tattoos to make "a look" much like others. No question, we will go to great lengths to receive the outside stamp of approval from those around us. Benjamin Franklin, one of this country's founding fathers, accurately described the condition this way:

> *The eyes of other people are the eyes that ruin us.*
> *If all but myself were blind, I should want neither fine clothes,*
> *fine houses, nor fine furniture.*

For some reason, we make the mistake of believing that what others think of us is more important than what we think of ourselves. When we do this, we diminish the unique individual that we are and take on the look and actions of those around us. To some extent, we seem to be willing to give up our own inside identity to have a life on the outside that meets the approval of everyone else. Obviously, being overly concerned about what others think is not a productive way to live.

So how can we become more focused on who we are on the inside?

Understand that you are unique for a reason.

Each of us has interests, abilities, motivations, and ways of doing things that collectively point our lives in a certain direction. We have been given these qualities for a reason. In other words, there is an intended purpose for our lives. Because it's not spelled out for us, we have to look inside and think carefully about what these interests and abilities are leading us to do. This is important stuff. If we are primarily concerned about what others think, it's much more difficult—often impossible—to determine what our inside lives are calling us to do.

Be willing to work to confirm your intended purpose.

Developing a meaningful life requires time and effort. You have to be willing to work at it. You may read your "life signals" wrong and have to restart, or you may encounter unexpected difficulties along the way. But, like any great athlete working to develop a skill or any dedicated doctor working to find a much-needed cure, you have to be willing to work to confirm your intended purpose. Letting other people's opinions distract you from this work is a poor choice indeed.

Remember, life's not about what you get, but what you give.

If there is a secret to life, it has to have something to do with helping others. Remember, we are here for each other. Therefore, as you focus on what's going on inside of you, keep thinking about how you might use your life to help others ... to make someone else's life better. Don't be distracted or changed by outside opinions. Think instead about who you are and what your life can do for others.

So, this bit of advice: focus your time and efforts on the inside ... on what your life is saying to you, and what you can accomplish with it. Regardless of your age or circumstances, you can do something very special with your life. But you have to look inside to determine what it is.

The Choice to
Activate the Goodness in Your Life

When it comes to the amount of goodness we see in other people, they are all over the map. Some people we know are great examples of goodness and always seem to be doing good and helpful things for others. We also know individuals who seem to have little or no goodness in them and, as a result, seldom, if ever, reach out to help someone in any special way. In other words, the contents of our "goodness tanks" vary greatly and range from being almost full to just about empty.

Why the differences in goodness between individuals?
The amount of goodness in our lives is determined by the choices we make. The more we choose to do good things for others—help a friend through a rough spot, support an associate's idea at work, improve the community, volunteer to tutor a child, and so on—the more our goodness tank contains. And while the amount of goodness in someone may be very small at the moment, there is always the potential for a significant increase. Even people who have made big mistakes, individuals who have wronged their family or friends in some way, even those who have lived their daily lives in self-centered ways … everyone has an opportunity to increase the level of goodness in their lives. It is totally dependent on the choices they are willing to make.

Why is this goodness so important?
Frankly, I've never seen or heard of any modern-day miracles. I am aware, however, of thousands of special things done by people for others: the fireman who saved the young child's life, the researcher who developed a much-needed vaccine, the man who set up a social media fund to help a destitute family, the people who volunteer to visit the shut-ins … the list goes on and on. These "miracles" were, in my view, performed by everyday people guided by the goodness

within them. It is through the goodness in our lives that you and I, in effect, have the opportunity to become "miracle workers" in this world. Without a doubt, you are potentially a lot more important than you may have ever realized.

And how do you activate this goodness, or increase it, in your life?

With your choices: There is a direct correlation between the quality of your choices and the level of goodness in your life. You have the stick, so to speak, and through your choices you control both the presence of goodness in your life as well as the amount of goodness you impart to others.

With your actions: While our choices define how we want to help, it is through our actions that our goodness is used to benefit others. Not just by thinking or talking about it, but by actually doing something to help. The idea is not to retain our goodness, but to use it to help others each day.

Through your life's purpose: Each of us possesses a unique combination of interests and abilities—our way of doing things, so to speak. These qualities help us determine our purpose in life. Our purpose will always have something to do with helping others. Therefore, this goodness is an indispensable quality not only to identify your purpose, but to use your life to benefit others in your own special way.

Will your goodness be challenged?

There will always be people who will push you to put your goodness aside and "have some fun" in life. But a meaningful life is not just about having fun. It's more about achieving a level of satisfaction: satisfaction that comes from living in a good and proper way, satisfaction that comes from using your life and your goodness to help others. You will encounter people whose suggestions will, if followed, diminish the amount of goodness in your life. But you can prevent being a victim of such influences. You can remain an independent thinker, be the leader of your life, and make the choices that are best for you. Once again, these are choices only *you* can make.

The Choice to
Forgive

Forgiveness is a process that starts with a choice—simply the choice to forgive. That choice may be reflected in an open disclosure that says "I forgive you" in some way. Or it may trigger a handshake or possibly even a hug. Such a choice starts the process of forgiveness … a process that may take some time to complete. The time required to forgive, however, can be shortened if we acknowledge three things:

First, acknowledge what is done is done.

If the deed is done, there is nothing we or others can go back and change. No question, some misdeeds are worse than others and the process of forgiveness may take longer or, in extreme circumstances, be near impossible to achieve. But in the vast majority of situations, the process can be initiated by accepting that the deed is done and making the choice to move on from there.

Second, acknowledge that we all make mistakes.

Whether it's our mistake or the other person's, no one is perfect and we shouldn't expect perfection from anyone. We have to offer the same acceptance of imperfection to others that we would like for others to give us. While we don't get up each day expecting someone to do wrong to us, we shouldn't be totally surprised when human errors and mistakes occur.

Third, acknowledge that the future can be much better if we forgive today.

We have to remind ourselves that if we "let it go" and move on, there is an opportunity—for us and others—to accomplish better things in the future. Extended or lifelong grudges seldom hurt the other guy but almost always create unhappiness in our own life. So, the process of forgiveness not only relieves us of this burden, it also sets the table for everyone to accomplish better things in the days ahead.

It takes a strong person to forgive, an individual who can mentally "rise above" the circumstances and see the benefit of moving past them.

The weak can never forgive.
Forgiveness is an attribute of the strong.

Mahatma Gandhi, *All Men Are Brothers*

And what about forgiving ourselves? We have a tendency to carry around our own mistakes for an extended period of time, especially if we've made a big one. We can mentally beat up on ourselves for years for something that we can never go back and change. Personal forgiveness, like that which we offer to others, starts with a choice ... the choice to forgive ourselves and work to live a better life. The three points apply to personal forgiveness as well, but the third one is of particular importance. We must focus our thoughts and efforts on accomplishing something better in the future if we want to start leaving the past behind today.

So, as you consider the role of forgiveness in your life, reflect on these three things: you can't change the past; all humans make mistakes; and your choice to forgive can lead to better things in the future. When you make the choice to forgive, you start to release the past and allow you, and others, to work toward better things in the future.

When you forgive, you in no way change the past.
But you sure do change the future.

Bernard Meltzer, *Guidance for Living*

It's important to remember that forgiveness is a choice we can put to good use every day. We encounter people daily who say or do something that offends us in some way. Rather than react to these small offenses and get upset, we should "pull out" our choice of forgiveness and silently use it right then and there. Letting some things go and simply forgiving without saying a single word can improve our lives and the lives of those around us. May you and I be willing to conduct ourselves in such a forgiving way.

The Choice to
Label Less and Love More

Many of us operate as people-labeling machines drawing vast conclusions about others based on how they look or how they talk. We overlook our own unique characteristics but are often quick to classify, sometimes even criticize, those who don't appear to be like us. We tend to group people based on external factors, and then—mistakenly—consider any member of the group to be like all the others.

One of our biggest labels is ethnicity. We group people based on the color of their skin or some special clothing they may wear. Whatever opinion we have of the group, right or wrong, carries over to the person in front of us even though we know nothing else about them. Religious groups are another big label we put on others. We don't fully understand our own religion, yet we'll "doom someone to hell" just because they don't believe what we do. Sexuality is another … it's none of our business, but we'll comment about someone anyway. And, of course, political groups—something's wrong with you if you don't see the role of government as I do.

It's amazing when you stop and think about it. We can form our entire opinion about someone based on these labels, having never met the individual or talked with them face to face. We seem to agree with the age-old teaching— "judge not that you be not judged" — but we fail to practice it in our daily lives. Almost every one of us is guilty of this type of ill-informed prejudice to some degree. But regardless of why we have come to be like this, labeling people is a very poor choice. It is much better to be an independent thinker who views people based on their individual characteristics and personal conduct, including how they treat those around them.

It's time we make the choice to look at the people around us as unique individuals capable of loving, caring, wanting, and working just like you and I. We have to remind ourselves that those around us may look different and be different, but most want to have an enjoyable life and accomplish something good with their lives just as you and I do. It's what's inside of a person that really counts. We simply need to stop being judgmental and pigeon-holing people based on the way they look. Today would be a good day to put your people-labeling machine away and never use it again. Steve Maraboli, author of *Life, the Truth, and Being Free*, gave us this perspective about the effect of judging:

> *Judging prevents us from understanding a new truth.*
> *Free yourself from the rules of old judgments*
> *and create the space for new understanding.*

So what is really important in forming our opinion of someone? There are many factors that come to bear on our view of another person, but the most important should be this: How they treat other people! Never mind that he is a great football player; how does he treat other people? Never mind that she's one of the prettiest women you've ever seen; how does she treat other people? Never mind that he's very successful in business; how does he treat other people? If someone treats other people in good and kind ways, it's almost a guarantee they are good and kind as well. American writer Henry James said:

> *Three things in human life are important: the first is to be kind;*
> *the second is to be kind; and the third is to be kind.*

So let's quit judging people based on some label we place on them. Let's work harder at becoming good and kind ourselves. After we accomplish that, we can then start to judge others on the very same basis: whether they are a good and kind person as well.

Clearly, we can use more good and kind people in this world. It's a label we should all be proud to wear.

The Choice to
Get Involved

There are many problems, some very significant, in our towns and cities that need to be addressed. But, as with all such issues, someone has to care enough to stand up, get involved, and go to work to change things, hopefully for the better. No question, most people will rally in support of a positive change, but it takes a willing individual to get things started so others can follow and become a part of the overall improvement effort.

When our conscience gets pricked by a call to action like this, we frequently avoid the challenge and the hard work by thinking: What could I possibly do? Well, nothing if you aren't willing to get involved and go to work to improve a situation. Many times, we don't know exactly what should be done until we commit, dig in, and become familiar with the details. But if there is a real need and thus a real opportunity to help people, we have to be willing to take the first step and to accept some risks, especially when major changes are involved. Norman Rice, the former mayor of Seattle, encouraged us to take such risks with these words:

Dare to reach out your hand into the darkness,
to pull another hand into the light.

In addition to mustering some courage, we have to remember that we are here for each other. Your life was never intended to be lived in a vacuum or away from the needs of others. Truth be told, it's not that difficult to identify a problem, a situation, or a circumstance that you could address and improve in some way. We feel these needs almost every day as we read the news online or talk about problems in the community with friends. There are problems right around you that could be addressed, maybe totally corrected, if you were willing to get involved. Reflect on these situations and think about the ones that move you the most, that upset you in some way. Think about one that tugs on your heartstrings, where you can see the people who need help. You'll never fix everything, but there are important needs out there where your life can make a difference.

Will there be disappointments? For sure, as real improvements are seldom easy. Will others question why you are doing what you're doing? There will always be doubters, but you're following the conviction of your heart, not what others are telling you to do. Will there be some failures? Most certainly; achieving important change can be a two-steps-forward, one-step-back experience. But knowing that you gave a portion of your life to make someone else's life better will be its own reward. Nelson Mandela, the South African anti-apartheid leader who was imprisoned for twenty-seven years for his efforts and later became the president of the country, explained what makes life count:

What counts in life is not the mere fact that we have lived.
It is what difference we have made in the lives of others that will
determine the significance of the life we lead.

Never doubt this for one second: you can make a positive difference in the lives of others. It doesn't matter that you don't have the resources; those can be found. It doesn't matter that you don't know everything you need to know; that can be learned. It doesn't matter that the problem is a big one; there will be others who will help. Don't just accept things as they are. You can change things and make life better for others if you make the choice to do so. It will not only change others' lives, but it's a choice that will change your life as well.

When you reach out to those in need, do not be surprised if the
essential meaning of something occurs.

Stephen Richards, *The Ultimate Power of Positive Thinking*

49

Section 3
Creating a Caring You

PERSONAL NOTES AND REMINDERS

*The
choices
we make today
will define our lives
tomorrow.*

4

DISCOVERING YOUR INTENDED PURPOSE

Granted, it's much easier and less stressful to live one day at a time and not worry too much about what we are *supposed* to do with our lives. Besides, it's pretty heady stuff to think that there is something specific we were put on this earth to do. Most of us aren't very anxious to go through the difficult process of determining why we are here. However, if we don't devote a significant effort to achieving this understanding, we will likely never discover the answer to this fundamentally important question: What is the intended purpose of my life?

But if we pay attention to our interests, our motivations, the needs of others, and the things that are pulling on our heartstrings—and think carefully about them—that purpose will, at some point, become clear to us. Here's a clue. Regardless of what your life's purpose turns out to be, it will have something to do with helping others. The topics in this section are provided to stimulate your thinking about your life's purpose and motivate you to think carefully about why you are here.

CHOICES ADDRESSED IN THIS SECTION

The Choice to

Understand Why We Are Here
Let Love Guide Your Life
Determine Who You Were Born to Be
Follow the Signals

The Choice to
Understand Why We Are Here

We've all had wishful moments about being some great person. For some reason, we have a tendency to think we need to achieve a certain level of fame and fortune to be important and make a difference in this world. As a result, we tend to focus on ourselves ... about the things we have, about how we look, and the degree to which we are accepted by those around us. Many of us fail to understand that living a meaningful and effective life is not really about us, but rather how we use our life to help others. Marcus Tullius Cicero, the Roman statesman and lawyer, summarized it this way:

> *"Non nobis solum nati sumus."*
> *(Not for ourselves alone are we born.)*

Granted, we have personal challenges and worries that influence our lives. Lack of money, insufficient education, health problems, family obligations, or some really poor choice we made years ago can be reasons we haven't accomplished as much in life as we would like. But maybe success in life has little or nothing to do with these things. Maybe there's another factor that really determines whether our life is a productive and special one.

There is one fundamental understanding that can enhance our lives significantly. It's this: Your life was not given to you just for your personal enjoyment. You are not here to live just for yourself, but to also use your life to help others. You are not here to *get* more but to *give* more. Coming to this basic realization can be a life changer. When you make the choice to adjust the focus of your life from exclusively helping *yourself* to also helping *others*, you change your life in a very significant way.

> *Being a man or a woman is a matter of birth.*
> *Being a man or a woman who makes a difference*
> *is a matter of choice.*
>
> Byron Garrett

You may think I'm splitting hairs here, but it's not our day-to-day activities that are important. What's important is how we use these activities to help others in some way. For example, it's not that important you are a banker: what's important is that you are a banker working to help others have a better life. And it's not that important you are a law-abiding neighbor: what's important is that you reach out to help your neighbor in need in some special way. It's not just what you *do*, but what you *do to help others* that is important.

In your own unique way, you can make other people feel special, feel cared for, and feel they are important. It's a caring that comes from your heart as you reach out to improve the lives of others. It is the act of giving ourselves to others that, in effect, makes us whole. Ralph Waldo Emerson gave us this perspective about approaching life this way:

It is one of the most beautiful compensations of this life that no man can sincerely try to help another without helping himself.

One of life's most important insights … we're here to help others have better lives. In doing so, we not only improve someone else's life, but we improve our life as well. Just try it. Reach out and start helping others in your own special way. Not only will your actions make them feel more love and care, but you will feel more love and care in your life as well. Interestingly, life works just the opposite from the way we typically think. It's not really about helping ourselves. It's all about using our life to help the other guy.

As two of her neighborhood friends sat in the pew waiting for Mary Wilson's funeral to start, one of them turned to the other and said, "Mary helped me so many times over the years. She was so special. She made me feel that someone in this world really cared about me. My life has been much better simply from the love and concern she gave me."

May more of us come to understand the importance of using our lives, not just for ourselves, but to do helpful things for others.

The Choice to
Let Love Guide Your Life

We can't make love happen. Instead, love just appears, awakens something inside of us, and takes over some aspect of our life. Suddenly we notice this wonderful feeling about someone we want to be with or something we want to do with our life. We didn't cause it to happen. But wow! There is love, adding another dimension to our life and, most likely, leading us off in some new direction. As these words from *The Prophet* explain, we are not in control of love or its entry into our lives:

> *And think not that you can guide the course of love.*
> *For love, if it finds you worthy, shall guide your course.*

Love can be the most important force we will ever experience. Love can lead us to our partner in life, to the work we want to do, to the support of a special cause, to correct a wrong in our community, to help the neighbor down the street, and much, much more. Almost everything we do in life that is of real value has "a love connection" to it. The challenge for you and me is to identify when love is at work in our lives and then make the choice to go where it is directing.

We can feel love, but what is it? This is an important question, something to stop and think carefully about. Love is the way our hearts guide our lives. We make most of our decisions "in our heads" in an effort to be logical and correct about things. But our hearts have a way of bringing special signals to our attention, offering insights and senses of direction that reflect who we really are and what we really feel. It's not uncommon for our heads to be telling us one thing while our hearts convey another. Which to follow is one of those very important choices that only you can make.

> *Let yourself be silently drawn by the strange pull*
> *of what you really love. It will not lead you astray.*
>
> Jalaluddin Rumi

Here are three questions that may help you bring love into greater focus within your life:

Are you hiding from your heart's influence in your life?

While we can't control love's entry into our lives, we can certainly hide from it. As powerful as love can be, its role is still subject to the choices we make. If we choose to treat those close to us in unkind ways or fail to help individuals we see in need, we are, in effect, hiding our life from the signals that love provides. Love can be a very powerful force, but our choices can cause us to ignore it.

Are you listening to what your heart is saying to you?

Sometimes love sends us important signals, but we fail to recognize love "knocking on our door." We are just too busy with our daily lives to stop and let love in. We can be so driven by our "to do" lists and the expectations of others that we're unable to hear love above all the noise and distractions in our lives. Make sure you take the time to listen and think carefully about what love is saying to you.

Are you willing to follow where your heart leads?

There are times when love has touched our lives and we have felt it with certainty, but we just aren't willing to make the choice to follow. We like the salary we are making now and aren't willing to accept less even though we know the other work is more important. We like living near our family and aren't willing to move halfway around the world even though the project is calling us to come. Love provides direction, but we are not always willing to follow.

To live under the guidance of love and to share our love with others are two of the most important choices we will ever make. We should let love guide our lives and be a factor in every important choice we make. Dr. Debasish Mridha, physician and author of *Verses of Happiness*, explained it with these words:

> To reach your destination,
> follow the directions of your heart.
> It knows the way.

The Choice to
Determine
Who You Were Born to Be

It is one thing to determine what you *want* to do with your life, but something very different to determine what you were *meant* to do. The former is low risk since we often tell ourselves, "If this doesn't work out, I'll do something else." The latter is high risk because if we miss the opportunity to utilize our own special gifts, we may spend our lives doing something we were never intended to do.

If you can't figure out your purpose, figure out your passion.
For your passion will lead you right to your purpose.

T. D. Jakes, Bishop of The Potter's House

We are very different from one another. One of us wants to be outside, the other indoors. One excels in math, the other in history. One wants to paint, another to sing. One wants to be a doctor, the other an engineer. We may be similar on the outside, but inside where it counts, we are very, very different.

It is through these differences that we help each other live more meaningful lives. For example, if everyone wanted to be a doctor, the wait at the doctor's office might be very short, but who would fix our cars, fly our planes, manage our grocery stores, paint our houses, teach in our schools, and so forth? In other words, it is our differences that make the world work. And our life works much better in this diversified world when we can find our intended purpose within it.

Confirming your purpose is a personal process that you choose to undertake for yourself. While other people may be helpful, the ultimate identification of your gifts—and what you will actually do with your life—depends almost solely on you. Something is going on inside of you … it's nudging you … it's pushing you … it's leading you in a certain direction. Your life is trying to speak to you and tell you what it wants to do. You have to find a way to listen and interpret what it is saying.

Where do these directional signals come from? I believe they come from our hearts. Our hearts "talk" to us in special ways and provide us with the motivation to utilize our gifts to help others. Why do I believe this? First, our personal interests and abilities emanate from deep inside of us. They may play out in external or physical ways, but it's the love in our hearts that reveals them to us and motivates us to amplify them within our lives. Second, it seems very logical to me to believe that we are here for each other. Accordingly, I believe we are given our "gifts" so that God's goodness can touch and benefit others in this world. As the Episcopal bishop Phillips Brooks reminded us:

No man has come to true greatness
who has not felt in some degree that his life belongs to [others],
and that what God gives him he gives him for mankind.

When I use the phrase "who you were born to be," do I mean that these gifts were given to you at birth and that your purpose was established from day one? No one can answer that question with absolute certainty. However, most parents agree that they could see certain likes and tendencies in their children from a very early age. Additionally, we start to recognize these preferences ourselves when we are very young. The key, however, is not when these "gift signals" started to appear but to make certain that, at some point in our lives, we understand what they are.

This is not simple or obvious stuff. And I can only tell you what I believe and have felt in my own life. You have to make your own choice whether you will listen to how your heart is directing you to your interests, your motivations, and the needs of others … or just work your life out "in your head." The better choice, by far, is to stop and listen carefully to what your heart is telling you to do.

You were born to be real, not to be perfect.
You are here to be you, not to live someone else's life.

Ralph Marston, The Daily Motivator

The Choice to
Follow the Signals

The subject of living out your purpose in life is addressed several times in this book. In part, because it's one of the most important choices we will ever make. And second, because many of us focus on "our job," never taking the time to determine what was really intended for us to do. So consider this question:

Were you brought into this world with certain intentions for your life, or were you just delivered here and left to work things out on your own?

Without taking the time to reflect on this question, you run the risk of never understanding why you are here. However, if you pay attention to the signals that enter your life—and are willing to make choices to support them—you don't have to stretch very far to realize that your life has a specific purpose, and that you, in fact, came equipped to fulfill it.

There are no specific steps we can follow to confirm our purpose in life. It's a journey we must each make for ourselves. It's up to each of us individually to process the clues we receive to make this determination. However, in doing so, there are three important indicators we can consider:

Our personal interests.

As we live our lives, we find ourselves motivated to do or be involved in certain things. When coupled with good choices, these interests can direct our lives in very specific ways. While such interests may develop though activities that take place externally, the motivation for them develops within us. It's our heart that reaches out, touches us in a special way, and confirms an important clue concerning the intended purpose of our life. Anthropologist and filmmaker Elizabeth Lindsey stated it this way:

*True navigation begins in the human heart.
It's the most important map of all.*

Our motivations.

When love enters and takes over our life in some way, we feel more alive. We become more energetic, more motivated, about things we want to do, people we want to be with, or visions of the future that we want to bring to fruition. Love, which is clearly centered in our hearts, can be the motivating force that leads us to our intended purpose in life.

The needs of others.

We are called to action by the needs of others. If we are alert to other people's needs, we encounter opportunities to activate our life in very special ways. Whatever your intended purpose turns out to be—one of thousands of possibilities—it will be connected to helping others in some way.

It's easier to go with the flow and just let your life work out in its own way. It's easier not to accept the responsibility for identifying and confirming your intended purpose, and instead just let life happen. But life doesn't just happen: it develops based on the choices you make. If those choices are not insightful and not well thought out, you are likely to live a life that was never intended for you. On the other hand, one of the most exciting feelings comes when a person has identified and is starting to live out their purpose in life. As Mark Twain explained it:

The two most important days in your life are
the day you were born, and the day you find out why.

Your personal interests, love directing you in some way, and the needs of others are all important signals leading you to your intended purpose in life. When you feel these pulling on you, be willing to make the choices that allow you to follow where they lead. You are here for a reason: your life has a purpose. Be willing to work—and think carefully—to confirm what it is.

Section 4
Discovering Your Intended Purpose

PERSONAL NOTES AND REMINDERS

*The
choices
we make today
will define our lives
tomorrow.*

5

HELPING OTHERS

There are people in all parts of the world—including in the very towns and neighborhoods in which we live—who need our help. Yes, we see many people reaching out to help others almost every day, but the actual needs of people extend well beyond what is already being done. Therefore, you and I should take stock of ourselves to determine how we are using our lives, and our choices, to make life better for someone else.

CHOICES ADDRESSED IN THIS SECTION

The Choice to

Be a Fan of Others
Water Someone's Life
Be Kind to Others
Do for Others

The Choice to
Be a Fan of Others

While recently attending a "celebration of life" dinner for a nine-ty-five-year-old who had just passed away, I witnessed one of the grandchildren stand and give his toast, saying, "You know, Nanny and Granddad were our family's biggest fans. No matter what, they always supported and rooted for us. They not only made us feel good … they made us feel important."

Those comments by this young man made me stop and think. I asked myself: Am I offering positive support to my family members and others around me who deserve to hear such words? Am I cheering them on? And, to you, the same question. Are you making those around you feel good about who they are and what they're doing? Chris Rock, the talented comedian, put the importance of these feelings in perspective for us with this statement:

There are only three things people need in life:
food, water, and compliments.

It seems that we are way too critical of others these days. We are quick to find fault but slow to offer our encouragement and appreciation. We have a tendency to quickly point out the negative things, yet slow to speak up when a positive comment is deserved or needed. But you and I don't have to be like this; we can choose to conduct ourselves in a more positive way.

It's important to note that the practice of being a fan doesn't depend on the other person. It depends on you and me, who we are on the inside, and our willingness to find some good no matter what. It has been said, "If another can easily anger you, it's because you are off-balance with yourself." So, if you and I are tilted toward the always-point-out-the-negative side of things, maybe this is a good time to right our ship and start looking for the good in other people.

Here are two suggestions you might find helpful as you work to become a more active and vocal fan of those around you:

Practice saying positive things to others.

Identify at least one good thing about the people you know, and in the coming weeks, make certain you compliment each one of them on it. You can even do this with people you encounter casually; for example, telling the grocery sacker, "My, you did a nice job sacking my groceries. Thanks so much!" You develop your compliment-giving skills just as great athletes develop theirs, by actually going out and practicing "the sport." So the more you practice, the easier and more natural being a positive and compliment-giving person will be.

Think about the impact your actions have on others.

We underestimate the importance of our role in helping others enjoy their lives. Remember, when you compliment someone, you actually touch their life in a special way and make them feel good. Compliments motivate people and help the recipients think positively about themselves. Leo Buscaglia, the professor and author known as Dr. Love, reminded us of our potential impact on others with this comment:

Too often we underestimate the power of a touch,
a smile, a kind word ... an honest compliment,
all of which have the potential to turn a life around.

Make the choice to be a fan of others and reach out and touch those around you in your own special way. And maybe someone will stand up at your celebration of life dinner and, as the young man did, say some nice words about the way you made them feel.

The Choice to
Water Someone's Life

Those of us who like to grow things know that there's a lot involved. We have to select our plants, purchase them, bring them home, plant them, fertilize them, and have some patience while they grow. A lot goes into living up to a green thumb reputation. But in spite of all this work and attention, there's one more simple—but very important—ingredient that determines the quality of life our plants will have. Without water, they will slowly die and wither away.

Well, our lives, and the lives of others, need water too ... "life water" as we refer to it here. This life water is created when we do something good or nice for someone. It is the feeling of caring, concern, or even love that is conveyed when we do nice things for others. It's pretty powerful stuff, as it can overshadow difficulties, make people feel instantly better, and even add new growth to the lives it touches.

We, in effect, create this life water by doing good and positive things for those around us ...

... by *smiling* and being friendly,

... by *calling* to let someone know we care,

... by *telling* our friends we appreciate what they do,

... by *hugging* our family members and saying thanks,

... by *stopping* and buying the homeless man lunch,

... by *volunteering* to help in our community,

... by *taking* an elderly person out for a ride,

... by *helping* someone financially if we can,

... by *doing* the little things that make someone's life better.

Interestingly, this life water helps the giver as well. Sharing such moments will help you grow in a number of ways. You will be happier. You will feel better about yourself. You will notice others feeling better about you. We don't often stop to think that we nourish our own lives when we focus our efforts on helping others, but it's true. Todd Stocker, author of *Turning Pain into Purpose*, explained it this way:

Helping others is the secret sauce to a happy life.

To put this watering work into action requires that you make the personal choice to get out your watering can (your life) and start using it to sprinkle others with goodness. This might seem like a small thing. But this activity is very important because it's through the efforts of everyday people like you and me that the world gets a little better, that lives are improved, that someone feels cared for ... that the watering gets done.

The quality of our lives and the extent to which we enjoy living them is dependent, in great part, on what we do for others ... to what degree we focus on others, not ourselves, and improve the life of another is some way. Attributed to Winston Churchill, it has been explained this way:

We make a living by what we get,
but we make a life by what we give.

This world needs a lot of watering right now. There are so many people who need your smile, your care, your concern, your love ... people who will benefit greatly from the life water you can provide. They will feel much better and grow in a very special way as a result of the watering work that you do ... and so will you.

Don't let your life dry up and blow away. Get out your watering can, and get busy.

The Choice to
Be Kind to Others

It seems like such a simple thing: being kind to those around us. You would think that such conduct would come naturally and we wouldn't have to be reminded about it. Yet we appear to be getting worse in this regard, becoming less kind to each other instead of more so. We witness politicians degrading one another. We hear of students bullying and being mean to others at school. We hear talk show hosts pointing out where people are "wrong-headed" in their thinking. And you and I ... we are slow to own up to our own faults, but often quick to announce the faults of others. Samuel Johnson, the English author, reminded us that we can choose to do otherwise:

Kindness is in our power, even when fondness is not.

Why does being critical of others seem to be increasing? One reason is that we are being conditioned to act this way by the many examples of unkind conduct we witness on the internet or in the news each day. Another reason, and possibly a bigger one, is because pointing out the faults of others gives us a feeling of superiority. For some reason, we think we are better and "in the know" when we say something unkind about another person. If we would focus on fixing ourselves and shaping up our own lives instead of pointing out where others fall short, we would make the world a much better place and be much happier while doing so. No matter what, we can be kind to others if we choose to. Roy T. Bennett, author of *The Light in the Heart*, passed along this reason for being kind to others:

Treat everyone with politeness and kindness,
not because THEY are nice, but because YOU are.

Here are a few things we should all remember regarding kindness:

Our role in life is not to criticize others, but to accept them as they are.

Even when we disagree, we should always do so in a respectful way. We accomplish so much more when we conduct ourselves in a way that clearly shows we care about the other person. No special exercise or diet is required to perform this feat … it's simply a choice that you and I can make.

We are not always right about what we think or say.

Seldom do we have all the facts or understand all the circumstances. As a result, seldom are we completely correct. Therefore, while we have our views and others have theirs, we can always treat others in a polite, respectful, and kind way. We can improve our life experiences by reaching out to people, not by lashing out at them.

We can't see what someone is feeling or thinking.

We don't know what the other person may be going through, or how they may be reacting to circumstances in their own life. Therefore, we must be careful not to overreact to someone's bad moments, but rather to be a living example to all around us of how to treat other people in a kind and respectful way.

If you can't say something nice about someone, don't say anything at all.

I can't begin to count the number of times my grandmother said that very statement to me, always in a loving way. She wanted me to be kind and respectful to others, and she would want you to be so as well. Granny was the best example of kind living I have ever known.

If our life is ever going to have a positive impact on others, we must choose to replace judgmental behavior with acts of kindness. Actor Josh Radnor reminded us how to be kind:

> It's not our job to play judge and jury, to determine
> who is worthy of our kindness and who is not.
> We just need to be kind, unconditionally and without
> ulterior motive, … especially when we'd prefer not to be.

The Choice to
Do for Others

There are many great examples of people reaching out to help others these days. In fact, there are millions of helpful works taking place throughout the country every day. To us, this is further evidence that God's spirit lives in everyone, and that many of us are heeding the influence of that spirit by using our lives to help someone in some special way. Such acts of kindness reflect an insight into how our lives should be lived. Albert Schweitzer, the German physician and Nobel Peace Prize winner, explained it this way.

The purpose of human life is to serve,
and to show compassion and the will to help others.

That said, there are millions of us who spend every day focused on ourselves. We have plenty to worry about. How on earth could we find the time to help someone else? Sure, we'd like to do more and we know there are people who need help, but we just don't have the time, or the resources, to do something like that. If this description fits you *in any way*, you should stop and think about how you are choosing to live your life. Leo Buscaglia, author of *Living, Loving, and Learning*, suggested living it this way:

It's not enough to have lived.
We should be determined to live for something.
May I suggest that it be creating joy for others,
sharing what we have for the betterment of person-kind,
bringing hope to the lost and love to the lonely.

Our lives are more meaningful when lived for others. Those who just live their life and never give this much thought tend, at some point, to look back and feel that their life didn't count for as much as they had hoped. Yes, we have our family circle that requires and receives our first allegiance. But to live life in a fuller way, we need to look beyond our immediate responsibilities to others who need food, shelter, love, or other small attentions that are missing from their lives. It is extending ourselves beyond our very own that adds another dimension to our life and sets a wonderful example for our family members and friends to follow. As indicated here, it's a way of life that *any* of us can adopt:

It doesn't take a lot of money.
There are dozens of people right in your community who have financial support, but are without the love and assistance that you can provide ... if you reach out to them.

It doesn't take a lot of your time.
You could devote some time each week, or a small amount each day, if you prefer, to do the small things that can make a really big difference in the lives of others.

It's not inconsequential to others.
It's absolutely amazing the positive feeling you can instill in someone lonely or in need simply by showing that you care about them.

It will make a major difference in your life.
You won't know the feeling until you experience it, but reaching out to people in need can make your life more worthwhile, even significantly change it.

> The best way to find yourself is to lose yourself
> in the service of others.
>
> Mahatma Gandhi

What will you choose to do for others? How will you help someone in need, someone whose life could be significantly enhanced by the care and concern you can provide? Without a firm choice to do something specific, your life will just move along as usual. But with such a choice you can make your life and the life of someone else more important, more meaningful, and more enjoyable in many ways. One little choice that makes such a huge difference ... will you make it?

Section 5
Helping Others

PERSONAL NOTES AND REMINDERS

The
choices
we make today
will define our lives
tomorrow.

6

GAINING KNOWLEDGE AND UNDERSTANDING

Being a knowledgeable individual gives you a significant advantage when there is an important choice to be made. In spite of this advantage, many of us don't have the basic knowledge or academic background we need. We either didn't have good educational opportunities as we grew up, or we failed to take full advantage of the ones that came our way.

But technology is changing the learning landscape as important educational experiences are now available via the internet. As only one example, Yale University now offers over forty courses, each consisting of twenty to twenty-five sessions, you can complete right at your computer, at your own pace, and at no cost to you. With many other educational resources available online at little or no charge, you can now take the route of self-education and become much more informed, if you choose to be so.

CHOICES ADDRESSED IN THIS SECTION

The Choice to

Be a Lifelong Learner
Become More Informed
Be Careful about Our Opinions
Gain an Understanding
Value Self-Education

The Choice to
Be a Lifelong Learner

Nothing in all the world is more dangerous
than sincere ignorance and conscientious stupidity.

Dr. Martin Luther King, Jr.

The truth is we're not as smart as we need to be.

We will stumble through a conversation trying to show that we know something even when we don't. We will make our point or take a stand on something although we don't have all the facts. Some of us will even maintain a "my way or the highway" position for a lifetime without ever taking the time to dig into the subject and cultivate a solid understanding of the issues involved.

Why is that? Why do we conduct ourselves in this way? It's because we believe that knowing—defined here as knowing more than the other guy—somehow lifts the value of our stock and improves our status among our peers. We think that being in the know is much better than the alternative. While this is certainly true, it's not something we can fake. You either know something or you don't. Being able to draw the line between the two will not only increase your favor among your friends, but it will also allow you to clearly identify what you need to learn.

Here's where our choices come into play again. We can find ourselves in one of these situations, maybe even embarrassed by our lack of knowledge about something, but typically when the conversation is over, it's over. We move on and forget about it. Instead, we should view these uninformed moments as creating an assignment for us to research, study, and learn more about the topic. This is easier to do if we choose to start viewing ourselves as lifelong learners, accepting the responsibility for educating ourselves throughout our lives. With the capabilities of technology today, the abundance of educational resources available via the internet, and the ability to search for something in a matter of seconds, teaching ourselves about any subject is well within our reach.

Five years from now you'll be able to find the best lectures in the world on the internet. It will be better than any single university.

Bill Gates in 2010

What are some of the benefits of becoming a lifelong learner?

Understand more about life and living.

Life, living, and the world can be complicated. The more we know, the better we will be in managing our life and the ways we choose to live it. It has been said that knowledge is power ... clearly it "boosts" our ability to make better and more insightful choices.

Become a more interesting person.

While being nice is very important, the more we know and can intelligently discuss and explain, the more interesting we become to our family, friends, and others. Knowledge is a key ingredient in our appeal to others.

Gain self-confidence.

Committing to a lifelong learning routine will improve how you feel about yourself as you expand your knowledge, and the more self-confident you will be. We enjoy life more when we have a reasonable level of confidence that what we're saying or doing is the right thing.

Learning is either a continuing thing, or it is nothing.

Frank Tyger, The Trenton Times

A commitment to lifelong learning will make you a better person, a better friend, a better employee, and a better contributor to your community and the world around you. The internet can bring almost every resource you need to your very fingertips. Make the choice to learn something new every day.

The Choice to
Become More Informed

Knowledge is free at the library.
Just bring your own container.

Unknown

Many of us find, as we move along in life, we need more education than we actually received. Maybe we didn't have the resources needed to obtain the formal education we wanted. Maybe we didn't apply ourselves and didn't work to take full advantage of the educational opportunities we had. Maybe we received a good education, but discovered later that we focused on the wrong thing. Regardless of our current circumstance, all of us should work to become more informed individuals.

Years ago, filling such a knowledge gap required that we go back to school, or learn from actual experiences gained from work and being out in the world each day. While these two sources still apply, technology has brought a whole new world of educational opportunities to us. Today, we can become highly informed individuals using our computers right from our homes or offices. There are literally hundreds of well-established educational websites that provide thousands of high-quality courses and presentations on a wide variety of topics ... and at virtually no cost to you and me.

As an example, TED Talks now offers more than 2,500 presentations by highly qualified individuals who have both academic and real-life experiences they share with you ... for free. You can select a topic of interest and become much more knowledgeable about the subject in an hour or so. Other examples include the University of Pennsylvania, Johns Hopkins, University of Michigan, Stanford, Duke, and many other universities that offer free courses online to those willing to invest their time and effort to become more informed. You will find hundreds of such educational opportunities on dozens of academic-related websites ... if you make the choice to search for them.

How do you develop a plan to become a more informed individual?

Consider your personal interests.
You have natural interests, the things that get your juices flowing and are important to you. These may be subjects you are personally interested in or topics that would help you be more informed at work. Make sure your education planning considers these.

Consider your personal conduct skills.
Your ability to show respect for others, to communicate effectively, and to practice good social skills will be major factors in your level of success in life. These are very important topics that should be included in your educational plan.

Consider your need for knowledge about America.
You live in a great country, but do you know how it became so and how it functions today? American history, American government, and the American economic system may not seem that important to you. But having a deeper understanding of each of these will help you become a more productive citizen.

I suggest you start with a notebook or computer file to have a central place to keep a list of the educational websites and presentations that interest you. You can record each educational experience and note points you've learned—your self-education record, so to speak.

Will you make the choice to become a more informed individual? Will you go to work to expand your knowledge about things in which you have a personal interest, the history and workings of America, and basic social skills that are important to everyone's success? Will you work to develop an educational plan tailored specifically for you? It's another powerful choice that only you can make.

Four years was enough Harvard. I still had a lot to learn,
but had been given the liberating notion
that now I could teach myself.

John Updike, Novelist and Literary Critic

The Choice to
Be Careful about Our Opinions

We are all entitled to our opinions, right? Well, maybe not. Here's what Harlan Ellison, author of *Dangerous Visions*, had to say about it:

> *You are not entitled to your opinion.*
> *You are entitled to your informed opinion.*
> *No one is entitled to be ignorant.*

Most of us have dozens of opinions, maybe even hundreds. We have opinions about friends and neighbors and how they should live their lives; about the towns we live in and the changes that should be made; and about politics and what is right and wrong about our country. We have opinions about what others think, what they believe, and how they view the world. We have opinions about clothes, food, cars, sports teams, TV shows, and on and on. Our list of opinions is a long one indeed.

And most of us feel strongly about our opinions. We sometimes take a strong stance when we discuss them with others. But shouldn't we stop and think about our opinions from time to time? Shouldn't we question whether we developed an independent opinion based on facts, or if we were "sold" our view by a friend or family member? Shouldn't we occasionally ask ourselves: Is my opinion about this well-informed ... or not? Tryon Edwards, compiler of the *Dictionary of Thoughts*, reminded us:

> *He that never changes his opinions, never corrects his mistakes,*
> *and will never be wiser tomorrow than he is today.*

As you think about your opinions, you might consider your answers to these questions:

Is my opinion supported by facts?
Almost every one of us is capable of developing a solid opinion if we know the facts. Unfortunately, many of our friends and almost

all of our politicians provide few actual facts these days. Plus, you and I are often lousy at doing our homework. We often accept things based on who is saying them, not on what is actually being said. As a result, many of us are walking around with emotional opinions, not factual ones.

Can I respectfully discuss my opinion with others?

We can learn a lot when we listen. But when our opinions are fueled by strong emotion or even anger, it is likely we will miss something. It takes a cool head to assess the information being presented and form a meaningful view and opinion. It takes a person willing to listen to the other side of the story to confirm or modify their own understanding.

How important is my opinion?

Obviously, some topics are relatively minor in the grand scheme of things. The fact that someone believes "Fords are better that Chevys" is not likely to change the world, or anyone's life for that matter. But if one believes that excessive federal debt could create significant problems for their children and grandchildren ... well, their opinion that we should have a balanced budget is a very important one. So opinions vary greatly in importance. As a result, we have to determine when we should just listen and when we should stand up and speak out for something that could make a real difference in some way.

Our opinions are really choices that we make over and over again ... each time the topic comes up. Like other things in life, good opinions depend on good choices. And we always have to be willing to listen and learn if we want to correctly confirm our opinion or change it in some way. Businessman Olin Miller put it this way:

To be absolutely certain about something,
one must know everything about it or nothing at all.

Think about your opinions ... be willing to change some, and to stand up for others.

The Choice to
Gain an Understanding

Frequently, we act like we know something when we really don't. For some reason we want to appear knowledgeable even when we are not. In a way, such conduct is an act of intellectual dishonesty and hinders our ability to build trust and relationships with others. Marshall McLuhan, the Canadian English professor who predicted the development of the World Wide Web, reminded us:

A point of view can be a dangerous luxury
when substituted for insight and understanding.

Remember, it's quite all right to say, "I don't know." Or, "I don't know if I should do that." Or, "I don't have all the information I need to make that choice." The folly is not in admitting that you don't know enough to make a comment or take some action. The folly is in making an important choice or statement when you don't have the real understanding to do so.

It takes a certain level of maturity, regardless of your chronological age, to admit that you don't know something. Acknowledging this lack of understanding is the first—and most important—step in actually achieving the understanding that you need. Being honest with yourself and others about what you don't know positions you to make the choice to obtain the information you need to become a more informed individual. It's actually acknowledging that you don't know or understand something that opens the door for you to learn and make improvements.

The father sat talking to his 16-year old son ... "There will be times in your life when you will have a major choice to make ... a life-defining choice that will set the overall direction of your life for years to come. Whatever you do, never make such a choice without gaining a solid understanding of your options and the decision you are about

84

to make. You can never know everything, but you can make sure you know enough to understand what you're about to do."

Making choices, especially important ones, without having a reasonable level of understanding about what you are doing is a foolish mistake. When it's your life you are dealing with and the consequences of a poor choice are potentially damaging, it will always be a wise investment to stop and take the time to collect the information you need to make an informed choice.

Don't pretend to know something when you don't. If you want to create a meaningful life, you have to take the time to obtain the information you need to make good decisions. There is no advantage to a quick choice or decision if it turns out to be a poor one.

If you need motivation to take your time to become more informed before making a certain choice, remember this. What later turned out to be a very poor choice, seemed to be a good one at the time we made it. What disqualified it as a good choice was the knowledge we gained from the actual experience. While experience will always be a good teacher, we can gain an advantage by doing homework beforehand and seeking out individuals who already have experiences they can share with us. If you're too quick to act, you may never have the opportunity for a do-over and the cost to you could be significant.

As this insightful bumper sticker reminds us:

*If you think education is expensive,
try ignorance.*

It's a fact. Informed people make much better choices than uninformed ones. So do your homework. Take the time to become more knowledgeable before you forge ahead and ignore potential consequences. If you do, your choices will be significantly better and your mistakes will be fewer and further between.

Become an informed choice maker ... it's the best way to go.

The Choice to
Value Self-Education

Never has there been a time in our country like there is now. More and more of us are willing to take a small snippet of information found on the internet and form our entire opinion based on it. We are changing from wanting fact-based information from informed sources to readily accepting opinion-based comments from almost anyone. As a result, if you believe what you hear or read each day—without stopping to be thoughtful about it—you will make more of your choices based on ill-informed opinions and fewer based on actual facts. Isaac Asimov, the Russian-born American writer, characterized the present circumstance this way:

> *There is a cult of ignorance in the United States.*
> *The strain of anti-intellectualism has been a constant thread*
> *winding its way through our political and cultural life,*
> *nurtured by the false notion that democracy means*
> *that "my ignorance is just as good as your knowledge."*

Why is this happening to us?

Influence of information on the internet.
People walk around with their heads in their phones being filled with no-fact opinions that do not help one to become a more informed individual. Talk is cheap, as they say, but it can be expensive if we let the wrong words influence our life in a significant way.

Lack of "big-picture" news reporting.
Instead of educating us with facts and accurate information about a situation so we can think for ourselves, most of our media outlets have become opinion mills slanting selective information to one side, their side, of the story.

Relaxation of academic standards.
We no longer require our schools to develop high levels of academic knowledge in our children. This may explain why the United

States has fallen from near the top only about fifteen years ago to 38th in math and 24th in science among the 71 countries tested by the 2015 Program for International Student Assessment.

Lack of knowledge about American history, government, and principles.
If someone doesn't understand the basic principles that have given rise to this country's development, they are more likely to make shortsighted choices that will change this country, but not in a good or favorable way.

Here's what we have in America today: *More and more ill-informed opinions being proliferated on an ever-expanding technology platform to fewer and fewer knowledgeable people.* If you and I are going to be effective choice makers, we need to understand these circumstances and how to deal with them.

What should you and I do?

We must wake up to the impact that the devaluation of knowledge is having on our lives.
Left unchecked, these circumstances will eventually damage our democracy and diminish the factors that have been fundamental to America's success. In fact, some changes are already starting to take place. We have to sharpen our choice-making skills to prevent these circumstances from impacting us.

We must take personal responsibility for educating ourselves.
Our schools aren't going to suddenly improve and the accuracy of the opinions we encounter each day will continue to decline. Therefore, you and I have to take the initiative to become more informed individuals on our own. Fortunately, the information we need is available to us. Dozens of universities and educational sites provide quality instruction at no cost. Good information is out there. You can educate yourself if you choose to do so.

A formal education will give you knowledge;
self-education will give you wisdom.

Dr. Debasish Mridha, M.D., Michigan Advanced Neurology Center

87

Section 6
Gaining Knowledge and Understanding

*The
choices
we make today
will define our lives
tomorrow.*

7

CONDUCTING
YOURSELF PROPERLY

I don't know the exact reasons why, but we see more and more people—both young and not so young—who don't know how to conduct themselves properly when out in public or when interacting with family members or friends. We could blame this "condition" on a number of things—poor parenting, improper influences coming via the internet, or friends and acquaintances who set bad examples on a daily basis. But since you can't change any of these things if they apply to you, you have to make the choice to manage your personal conduct in an effective way.

The advantage of doing so is this ... you can accomplish so much more with your life if you conduct yourself properly. And doing so is not that complicated. It requires a solid understanding of proper personal conduct, an adequate amount of self-control, and the willingness to make choices each day to live your life in a respectful and proper way.

CHOICES ADDRESSED IN THIS SECTION

The Choice to

Apologize
Ask Questions
Be Cell Phone Smart
Behave Yourself
Listen
Communicate
End the Argument
Compromise
Be Less Judgmental
Be Friends with Someone Different
Speak and Write Effectively

The Choice to
Apologize

I didn't start the thing ... why should I apologize?
I was trying to be nice about it ... it's not my place to apologize!
I know I'm right ... there's no need for me to apologize!

Regardless of the circumstances that sparked opposing viewpoints or fueled an outright argument, we tend to think that we were the one who was right and the other person was wrong. We are frequently reluctant to admit that we were wrong in some way. But does fault really matter when making the choice to offer an apology to end a disagreement? Does it really matter who or what caused it when we choose to apologize and put a difficult situation to rest? It doesn't. An apology is a tool of reconciliation that can, in fact, be used by either party.

Some people believe apologizing is a sign of weakness. They say you and I should be hesitant to apologize because it's a sign that we were wrong. But that's not true. It takes a strong person to apologize, especially when the point at hand was not clear-cut. Apologizing requires not only strength, but also a smart person ... someone who can recognize that the objective is not to establish who was right and who was wrong, but to put the matter to rest and move on with life.

Apologizing is an effective way to end a disagreement and, in many cases, to preserve an important friendship. Saying things like, "Thank you!" or, "I appreciate what you did!" are endearing comments that enhance the connection between two people. But saying, "I'm really sorry for what happened" ... regardless of who was right and who was wrong ... has an even stronger impact on the relationship. That's because its underlying meaning is, "I want to be friends with you!" Such a feeling is welcomed by almost everyone. Canadian cartoonist Lynn Johnston gave us this helpful perspective about the effectiveness of an apology:

An apology is the super glue of life.
It can repair just about anything!

If who was at fault doesn't really matter, what does? These three things:

Your sincerity.

For an apology to work, we have to be sincere about it. Thinking about the importance of the friendship or the connection between you and the other individual—not the subject of the disagreement—will help motivate you to offer a sincere "I'm sorry" to someone.

Your timing.

It's almost never too soon to apologize. Most people require some time to think about the circumstances before they see things better and understand the need for an apology. But as soon as you can be sincere about your feelings, go for it. The sooner the better, but it's never too late to apologize.

Your words.

Giving an excuse or reason, valid though it may be, for why the disagreement developed in the first place never works. You just have to be honest and simple with your apology, because it's the basic apology that seals the deal, not an explanation of why it happened in the first place.

Add a willingness to apologize to your people-skills toolbox. This is a tool that you will likely use many times during your life. The better your skills in using it, the stronger the friendships you will have. Mark Matthews, author of *The Protector* and *The Calling*, explained it this way:

*Apologizing does not always mean you're wrong,
and the other person is right.
It just means you value the relationship more than your ego.*

The Choice to
Ask Questions

Most of us aren't that interested in asking questions. We place more value on what we have to say than on listening to someone else. So, since asking questions gives others more opportunities to talk and less for us to do so, why should we consider it to be another important choice to make? Here's why:

Asking questions enhances our effectiveness in interacting with others.

Going through life as a big talker and a poor listener is not going to help you create good relationships or motivate others to want to be in your company. Granted, you and I need to have something to say, but equally as important, we have to understand the importance of asking questions in the overall communications process. We have to walk both sides of the conversational street if we want to be welcomed company by our family, friends, and others we may meet.

Asking questions shows your interest in the other person.

We should note that asking questions adds another dimension to our ability to listen. Appropriate questioning indicates "I am interested in what you have to say." Asking questions kindles a feeling within the other individual that you care about them and value what they offer. Asking questions indicates you think the person is important ... a nice stroke that is welcomed by almost everyone. You may impress someone intellectually with something you have to say, but, as silly as it may sound, you touch someone emotionally with the questions you ask. David Whyte, the poet who wrote about their importance, explained the benefit of asking questions this way:

The marvelous thing about a good question is that it shapes our identity as much by the asking as it does by the answering.

Asking questions sets up opportunities for you to learn something. It may be a point of information that you did not know; it may be an insight, a perspective, or point of view that you had not considered. Or rather than the information itself, it may provide you with an opportunity to find out what this person believes and what they are all about. While your questions can have a favorable impact on the other person, their answers can teach you things as well.

Asking questions is the polite and proper thing to do. Just like making good eye contact, not interrupting someone, and saying "please" and "thank you" are proper things to do, so is asking questions. If you want to be an individual who is adept socially, asking questions should be a skill that you develop. Current-day social norms are pushing us away from understanding the importance of being a *lady* or a *gentleman*. In fact, you may even object to those terms. But individuals who are skilled at conducting themselves in polite and proper ways will always enjoy an advantage over those who lack such abilities. As you review the items on your personal conduct list, make sure that asking questions is included. The importance of doing so is described rather well by Naguib Mahfouz, a winner of the Nobel Prize for Literature, when he said this:

> You can tell whether a man is CLEVER by his answers.
> You can tell whether a man is WISE by his questions.

Asking good questions will help others feel favorably toward you, increase your level of understanding, and enhance your social performance. Your questions must be appropriate for the moment, but practicing good questioning skills will improve the feelings of all involved and create environments for relationships to develop. It's a choice that requires a rather small investment, but can produce big returns.

Asking questions … it's a choice that all of us should make.

The Choice to Be Cell Phone Smart

It seems that almost every place you go these days there are people with their heads down, phones in hand, "carrying on life" via their cell phones. There are now more cell phones in the United States than there are people. Clearly, our daily routines are highly dependent on these little devices, smart phones as we call them. But the question we should ask ourselves is this: Are we being smart in the way we are using them?

Cell phone usage impacts our lives in three ways: physically, mentally, and socially.

Physically.

Doctors point to a new physical condition— "text neck" they call it—as evidence that extended cell phone usage can be physically deforming. When we stay in that hunched position two to four hours a day, it can curve our posture and cause back problems as well. The head weighs ten to twelve pounds upright, but when we lean over the thirty degrees or so for typical cell phone usage, the effective weight increases to over forty pounds. Over time, that can make us a member of the "text neck" crowd. Here's a suggestion. Make the choice to get your phone off your waist or stomach, hold it out more, and stand/sit straighter when you use it.

Mentally.

Many of us receive almost all our daily information through the internet via our phones. While much of this information can be good and helpful, some of it can contain ideas and thinking that are not in our best interest ... that influence us in poor or improper ways. The idea in life is to maintain a certain level of independence and to think for yourself. But the information flowing from your smart phone reflects other people's opinions, crowd thinking, and topics trending today. If you aren't careful, that little device in your hand can brain-wash you and make you more of a crowd thinker than an independent one.

Socially.

Few things are more annoying than someone talking on their cell phone in a public place. You are trying to have a nice meal with your friends when the guy ten feet away engages in a loud conversation. Clearly, he—and you when you are the one receiving the call— should step out of the public place to complete the conversation. Or someone is texting while sitting with a group of people who are verbally engaged. When you do this, it makes the other people feel like you don't care about what they have to say. Have some manners, get up, and step away if you have a call or text that must be handled.

I have to share this little story ... as I sat in a nice restaurant enjoying a special lunch with my wife and some great friends, I could not help but notice a young couple sitting next to us. Instead of talking to each other, they both had their heads down, hunched over their smart phones. Normally, this would not have aroused my feelings on this subject, but my gosh ... it was Valentine's Day, a time to look each other in the eye, exchange some meaningful conversation, and maybe even say, "I love you."

It's important to note that every day presents us with opportunities to have meaningful interactions with those around us, to hear what they have to say, and to share our thoughts and feelings with them. This is nearly impossible to do when we act like our phone is more important than they are.

Want to put your phone away and pay attention to those talking to you? There's an app for that — it's called RESPECT.

I promise you, the best moments in your life won't come via text, but rather when someone touches you with their words, with their expression, with their smile, with their feelings in some special way. Make this important choice: to text less, and listen and talk more. You may develop a connection that is special indeed, a connection you will never find on the internet.

The Choice to
Behave Yourself

No matter what, you and I can do the right thing. No matter our age, background, education, or circumstances, we can conduct ourselves in a responsible way. Even when we encounter a difficult situation—one with which we totally disagree—we can act and work in an intelligent manner to make things better. But many times, we do just the opposite. Instead, we act in foolish and impolite ways. In short, we don't behave ourselves. Forrest Gump classified such actions for us when he explained:

Stupid is as stupid does.

Forrest was right. It takes a smart person to manage themselves and do the right thing regardless of what others around them are saying or doing. Having a strong conviction about something is not an excuse for loud or improper behavior. No matter the topic or what others are doing, we can conduct ourselves in a responsible way.

Most of us don't realize that we are slowly being brain-washed to behave badly. Social media is training us by providing an almost unlimited number of examples of bad behavior. It's become way too easy to make a derogatory comment or give an ill-worded critique of someone in today's overly connected world. We experience so many of these negative expressions in posts, tweets, texts, and emails, possibly creating some of them ourselves, that we are being conditioned to believe that acting in a crude or unbecoming way is "normal."

Moving away from such negativity and back in a better direction depends on some good choices. We can choose to keep our mouths shut, take our fingers off our keyboard or phone, and think about things before we say or do something that we shouldn't. Most of us are very capable of conducting ourselves in a proper way—behaving, that is—if we just take the time to consider our actions before we take them and give ourselves an opportunity to make a better choice.

The crazy thing about this type of negative behavior is it hurts us far more than the other guy. We think we can somehow lift ourselves up by tearing someone else down. That's just the opposite of how life really works. You and I will never accomplish anything worthwhile on the back of another person. We can only do so by living our life in a good and helpful way and helping others achieve the same.

Every man is valued in this world as he shows by his conduct that he wishes to be valued.

Jean de la Bruyere, French Writer and Moralist

We all make mistakes and do things we wish we hadn't done. But there is no eraser in life that allows us to go back and change something that has already happened. Instead, we have to think about the future and decide how we will conduct ourselves from this day forward. It's an important choice that we can make ... to conduct ourselves in a proper and respectful way, no matter what.

So, before you fly off the handle, before you shout out at that other person, before you text that hurtful message ... stop and think for a minute. Consider whether your impending conduct will make things better or worse. In fact, you can establish a personal "ground rule" such as this to guide you:

As you live your life, you will encounter many opportunities to do a reactionary, or as Forrest characterized it, stupid thing. In fact, most of us encounter situations almost daily that test our ability to remain calm. The key to managing your conduct is not to wait until one of these testy moments happens, but to decide ahead of time how you will react. Long before you are "in the arena," even now as you read these words, you can make the choice to establish a personal ground rule concerning how you will conduct yourself at times like these. Here's an idea of what that ground rule might be: "Unless I'm threatened with physical harm, I will not overreact to others, but will conduct myself in polite and respectful ways ... even when others do not."

Before you act in a foolish way, make the choice to use your ground rule ... and behave yourself.

The Choice to
Listen

We love to talk ... but to listen, not so much. There are many reasons why we act this way. The main one being that we feel more important when we are doing the talking. Also, for some psychological reason, we mistakenly believe that the other person is interested in what we have to say ... even when we don't feel that way about what they offer in return. If we are going to become effective listeners, we have to start by recognizing that listening doesn't come naturally. We have to work to develop our listening skills. Stephen Covey, in his book *The 7 Habits of Highly Effective People*, explained our typical behavior this way:

Most people do not listen with the intent to understand; they listen with the intent to reply.

So, why should we want to be good listeners?

First, listening creates an invisible bridge that helps us build and maintain relationships. People can tell when we are sincerely listening to them and when we react with interest to what they have to say. As a result of being listened to, a person feels a connection with us, and the relationship or friendship is enhanced. Second, we learn and retain more when we focus and listen carefully to what is being said. Good listeners, over time, tend to know more and have better relationships than those of us who don't pay that much attention. Third, it's the polite and respectful thing to do. If we want to conduct ourselves in a proper manner and exhibit good personal conduct, listening is a very important part of the package. American financier and investor Bernard Baruch gave us one of the best reasons for being a good listener:

Most of the successful people I've known are the ones who did more listening than talking.

How do we become better listeners?

Develop a solid respect for the importance of listening.
Being a good listener will get you further in life than the ability to be a good talker alone. The better you are at listening, the more you will understand and the closer your relationships with others will be.

Become adept at asking questions.
As you talk with someone, instead of mentally preparing your next comment, develop a question instead. The better you are at asking questions, the better listener you will be. Make it a point never to leave a conversation without having asked a question or two.

Add listening to your people-skills package.
We know that such things as smiling at someone, shaking hands with them, having good eye contact, and greeting them in a respectful way are all parts of a good people-skills package. After the initial use of these skills, listening becomes the most important.

Maybe the real secret to being a good listener is to put yourself in proper perspective or balance with those around you. Unfortunately, many times we view ourselves as being a little more important than the other guy. That's always a mistake. Without question all are created equal. Regardless of who the other person is and what their station in life might be, you should value the fact that your lives have come in contact with each other. Therefore, you should *always* make the very best of the moments you have to personally interact with another individual.

So, keep your It's-Time-For-Me-To-Listen button handy.

And make sure you push it many times each day.

The Choice to
Communicate

We tend to think that the broader our vocabulary, the better our ability to communicate and the more interesting others will deem us to be. While there may be a bit of truth in these sentiments, the key to being an effective communicator is not in using big and fancy words, but in how you make the other person feel when you talk to them. If they feel you're not really interested, it matters little what you say or the words you say it with. On the other hand, if the person feels that you are sincerely interested in them, you almost instantly become more important in their life. Peter Drucker, the well-respected management consultant and author of *Innovation and Entrepreneurship*, explained it this way:

> *The most important thing in communication*
> *is hearing what isn't said.*

Obviously, consistent eye contact, careful listening, and asking questions are very important in establishing good communication with another person. When you look directly at someone, you send a silent signal that you are focused on them and what they have to say. When you listen and show that you are doing so, you advance the connection that you're developing. And when you ask questions in response to what they say, you, in effect, are verifying that you are on board with the conversational journey you are sharing. If you can honestly and sincerely connect with someone on all three of these pathways, you are *communicating* something that entails much more than words and can quickly turn strangers into friends. Henry Ford, the founder of the automotive company that bears his name, gave us this communications insight:

> *If there is any great secret of success in life, it lies*
> *in the ability to put yourself in the other person's place and to*
> *see things from his point of view.*

And, there are those special little words ... *please, thank you,* and *you're welcome.* We underestimate the strength of these little words, and, although they don't create great fanfare when they are used, they round the edges of an exchange. They make any conversation take on an element of kindness that, in a small but important way, endears the person using them to others.

If we want to be effective communicators, it's important to use the other person's name. When you do this, you have their undivided attention for the next several seconds. What happens when we hear our name may be difficult to explain, but there is no question that you receive a higher level of attention when you address someone by their name. "Michael, how have you been?" impacts me in a greater and more sincere way than "Hey, how have you been?" People like to hear their name and to receive comments addressed specifically to them so make it a practice to inject the other person's name periodically in the conversation. Dale Carnegie, the developer of self-improvement courses and author of the international bestseller *How to Win Friends and Influence People*, explained the significance of using a person's name:

A person's name is to that person
the sweetest and most important sound in any language.

There's more to being an effective communicator than the words that come out of our mouths. Yes, the words have to be understandable and make sense to impact us in some way. But how you make the person feel when you are delivering them is even more important. It's not just what you say, but how you say it that really counts. It's not just about words; it's about feelings. Show a person that you really care about them, and they'll be pleased they had the chance to communicate with you.

The Choice to
End the Argument

Have you ever been involved in a conversation that suddenly got out of hand? Have you ever become involved in a heated discussion with someone whose view seemed to be the very opposite of your own? We've all been in disagreements with someone. These situations can heat up, cause tempers to flare, and turn into outright arguments. The problem with arguments, however, is this: The more arguments you win, the fewer friends you will have.

In other words, you can be right about your point or the topic at hand, but damage the relationship by arguing with someone. So, before you walk into another argument, maybe you should stop and think about the downside of arguing and the upside of managing yourself, and the other person, around such a situation. Here are four questions that, if you consider the answers carefully, will help you take the high road the next time you see a verbal altercation coming your way.

Why do people argue?

People argue for two basic reasons. One, of course, is that they have differing or opposing views about something they deem important. But another, and possibly the greater reason, is the fact that those involved don't have sufficient control over their emotions to discuss the matter in a courteous, respectful, and intelligent way.

What is the result of most arguments?

Most arguments, at best, end in an un-officiated tie. Since typical arguments do not have independent referees or a way to keep score, most arguments end somewhere near where they began ... with each party clinging to their belief and considering the other guy wrong. The outcome of most arguments is left to individual opinions, the very things that started the argument in the first place.

How can you prevent getting into an argument with someone?

The answer here is very simple: just ask questions. Not in a sarcastic way, but with an honest desire to understand the other person's point of view. In other words, hold off on trying to make or enforce your point until you know and understand what the other person is saying about theirs.

How can you end an argument once you're in the middle of one?

You have to exhibit maturity and self-discipline to make this work. But if you discover that the other person is right, tell them so ... "I never thought about it that way, but you're right on this one." Or, if it's apparent that no one is going to change their mind, politely bow out ... "I want to think about this and do some homework."

Just remember, you can make the choice to end an argument. That doesn't mean you concede your point. Rather, it means that you take the initiative to talk in a calmer voice, to ask questions so you can understand the other person's view, and to discuss the matter in a more mature way. Rumi, an ancient Persian poet, left us with this very helpful reminder about arguments:

> Raise your words, not your voice.
> It is rain that grows flowers, not thunder.

It's not an easy thing to do, but you can make the choice never to argue again. Rely on knowledge and facts, not raised voices and baseless accusations. And, always be open to the possibility that the other guy may know exactly what he's talking about. As Miguel de Unamuno, the Spanish poet and philosopher, explained:

> A lot of good arguments are spoiled by some fool
> who knows what he is talking about.

If you're going to be an argumentative fool, it's best to be a very knowledgeable one.

The Choice to
Compromise

As most of us know, there are at least two sides to every story. Although we know this, we're not quick to be open-minded when we find ourselves in a discussion involving opposing views. We tend to stick to our viewpoint, unwilling to let someone convince us to think differently. André Gide, winner of the Nobel Prize in Literature, gave this view of such circumstances:

> *Most often people seek in life occasions for persisting in their opinions rather than for educating themselves.*

The problem with living in a stubborn way is that we are seldom all right or all wrong. The truth is usually some combination of perspectives, but it takes a spirit of conversational cooperation to work out what that is. Our perception that we know what we're talking about often hinders our ability to listen to the other view. But when we do, two important things happen. First, we learn something, and, second, we show respect for the other individual.

Whether it's in individual conversations or discussions with groups at work, school, or play, we need to be mindful that we will encounter opposing viewpoints—ideas and even outright recommendations that differ from our own. The question at a time like this is, How do we handle it? What do we do to make sure that we can see both sides and are creating an opportunity for a better understanding to develop? Here are some suggestions that will help you handle these situations, maybe even reach a compromise in the process.

Be polite.
Always show respect for the other person, talk in a normal tone, and conduct yourself in a professional manner. You can think so much better when you conduct yourself this way.

Focus on the facts.
There may be many opinions, but typically there is only one set of facts. If you focus on the facts and minimize the opinions, common ground can likely be found and shared.

Listen carefully to what others say.

It requires extra effort to fully understand the other view. When we're too emotional, it's difficult for us to hear, much less understand, what the other person is saying.

Ask questions.

When trying to understand a different view, polite questions are extremely helpful. It is through effective questioning that we are able to obtain a clearer understanding of another's view.

Present the logic of your position.

Facts are important, but the logic behind them even more so. Being logical aids the overall situation, and gives the opportunity to present your position more convincingly.

Be willing to adjust to reach agreement.

A combined conclusion is always stronger than any single opinion. Be ready and willing to work to find the logic in both positions and forge the middle ground.

> *Compromise is not about losing. It is about deciding that the other person has just as much right to be happy with the end result as you do.*
>
> Donna Martini, Wellness Advocate and Activist

A compromise is a choice to take some of your thinking and some of the other person's and combine them into an overall solution or view that is better than either could develop alone. If there is one thing we need in this country right now, it's men and women, particularly those in elected positions, who will work together logically to achieve things that are good for everyone. We need to take a more compromising approach to our everyday lives.

It's a choice you and I—and many, many others—should definitely make.

The Choice to
Be Less Judgmental

We are quick to form opinions about people, sometimes simply based on what we see ... how they are dressed and generally what they look like are typically all we need to draw a conclusion. We also are quick to judge people we've just met. We don't really know facts and details about these people, but we judge them anyway. Richelle E. Goodrich, writing in *The Beauty of Ugh*, gave us this insight about being fooled by what we see:

Eyes, so easily deceived, might judge more rightly with lids closed, allowing ears and hearts to remain wide open.

And technology is not helping our overly judgmental condition. We'll accept a text, tweet, or social media post and let it influence us far more than it should. We read something on the internet, unverified though it may be, and out pops our opinion as well. Almost unnoticed, we transfer this judgmental behavior to our interactions with others. We look at the lady in the grocery line and, based on the size of her body and the items in her cart, decide what type of person she is. It's a bad choice and a very poor way to conduct our lives, but we do it anyway. Writer Traci Lea LaRussa warned us about such short-sighted conclusions:

There is usually a side you have not heard,
a story you know nothing about,
or a battle being waged that you are not having to fight.

How can we stop being so judgmental? Granted, it's a difficult thing to do. But here are four points to keep in mind as you work to be less judgmental in your daily life:

The real person is on the inside.

It's impossible to assess a person by seeing them from afar or even meeting them for the first time. We have to get to know a person and understand what they're all about to form a valid opinion. Until we do, we should keep it in neutral and refrain from any judgments.

It's not our place to be judgmental.

The Bible tells us to "judge not that you be not judged." We don't want the people we encounter each day to be judging us ... no, definitely not. Therefore, this instruction is for us to offer the same courtesy to others that we want for ourselves.

Life works better for those who aren't judgmental.

The impression we make is much better when we are open and accepting of other people. When we look for the good in others as we go about our daily routine, we are happier, typically have more friends, and, over time, accomplish so much more.

It's more productive to judge ourselves.

Shouldn't we think about our own shortcomings and correct them before thinking about the shortcomings of others? The answer is, of course, yes. Each of us needs to improve in some way. Therefore, we should get our own house in order before judging others.

Steve Maraboli, writing in *Life, the Truth, and Being Free*, gave us this perspective:

> *How would your life be different if you stopped making negative judgmental assumptions about people you encounter? Let today be the day you look for the good in everyone you meet and respect their journey.*

You will need to give this choice some careful thought and serious effort if you want to live in a non-judgmental way. It's just too easy to do otherwise. But your life will be so much better if you simply look for the good in other people. And remember, you have to look inside to find it.

The Choice to
Be Friends with Someone Different

*Of all the things which wisdom provides to make life
entirely happy, much the greatest is the possession of friendship.*

Epicurus

Have you ever been to a social event and not known a single person there? You look around the room trying to find someone you might have something in common with, a like-minded soul with a similar view of life. No luck. You are starting to wonder if you should have accepted the invitation in the first place. You wish you could just leave, but after telling yourself that's not the proper thing to do, you take a closer look, and tell yourself, *I don't think there's anyone here like me.*

You visually hurry past the lady with blue hair and the guy speaking rather loudly about politics ... *I won't have anything in com-mon with those two.* You don't dare approach that young man you see ... *Kids operate on a different wave-length these days.* And those people over there near the wall ... *That's a different ethnic group, no way for me to just walk up to them.*

But what if you did? What if you made the choice to introduce yourself to these people and talk to them for a bit? *Well, I'm here, might as well try to make the best of it.* So off you go.

After shaking hands, you start listening to the loud guy with obvious political persuasions, and as you do, you realize he actually has a good point. You didn't know as much as you thought about that topic. You make a mental note to do a little more research on the subject when you get home.

After sitting down next to the blue-haired lady, you discover she is about to go through chemo and just wanted to get out this evening and do something fun. She turns out to be very funny and, in spite of the difficulty she is facing, has a great perspective about life. She inspires you so much! You make a mental note to check on her next week.

You introduce yourself to "the kid" and, after an interesting discussion, find the young man to be one smart cookie. His logic for not being part of the drug scene was very well stated and ... well, you plan to pass his insights along to some family members very soon.

And with your courage on the rise you head right over to the group in the corner that is obviously very different from you. To your absolute amazement, you were pulled right into that circle and had so much fun talking to them ... what nice people!

"Wow!" you're thinking as you depart. "Those were some really great folks." You were very surprised to find that these people—yes, different from you—were really interesting and had something important to share: an informed political view, a perspective about handling difficulties in life, an important insight about drugs, and a level of friendliness you had never experienced before. Sometimes we get all caught up in ourselves and fail to extend our hand and say hello to someone who is different from us. When we make a choice like that, we miss out on some very important moments in life.

Getting to know people who are different from you will help you become a more open-minded, informed, and accepting individual. You may be surprised what can be achieved when you simply share life and experiences in an open and honest way with someone who is different from you. Jodi Picoult, in *House Rules*, provides an insight that ties right in to the point we're making here:

It's never the differences between people that surprise us.
It's the things that, against all odds, we have in common.

View those who are different from you as opportunities for you to learn and grow. Make the choice to walk right up, introduce yourself, and get to know more about them. They'll add new perspectives to your life and you to theirs as well. We are here for each other. Don't miss the opportunity to share your life with someone who is different ... well, at first you thought they were.

The Choice to
Speak and Write Effectively

Listening may be our most important communications skill, but verbal and writing skills are right there with it. Listening positions you to respond well to others. But talking and writing well round out your ability to engage in meaningful communications with others. These skills are factors in the quality of your relationships, the effectiveness of your school or work activities, and your day-to-day life. Ellen DeGeneres warned us how these skills are being impacted in her book *Seriously ... I'm Kidding*:

> *What's not so great is that all this technology is destroying our social skills. Not only have we given up on writing letters to each other, we barely even talk to each other. People have become so accustomed to texting that they're actually startled when the phone rings.*

Whether we ever had good verbal and writing skills, we should note that technology and texting are working against our ability to improve them. Whatever your current proficiencies might be, your verbal and writing skills are under pressure and likely to get worse. Therefore, it's going to take very specific choices on your part to improve them. Mireille Guiliano, the French-American author and former CEO of Clicquot, explained the importance of these skills this way:

> *Intelligence, knowledge, and experience are important and might get you a job, but strong communication skills are what get you promoted.*

To set yourself up for improvement, you need to acknowledge two things. First, technology is not going away, nor will it become less functional. Therefore, you have to learn how to use technology in a positive and beneficial way. Second, if you have difficulty in speaking correctly or writing properly, you should upgrade these skills. If you can't achieve an above-average rating in your speaking and writing skills, you are not likely to have above-average success in life. Here are a few suggestions:

To improve your use of technology ...
- Email in complete sentences with proper punctuation.
- Text in whole, correctly spelled words.
- Excuse yourself when taking a call or talking on your phone.
- Put your phone away when conversing with others.

To improve your verbal communication skills ...
- Ask three friends to describe your verbal skills honestly.
- Make sure you are listening as much as you are talking.
- Incorporate questions into every extended conversation.
- Always think of your conversations as two-way streets.

To improve your written communication skills ...
- Always write thank you notes. Never email them.
- Write and mail at least one letter each week to someone you care about.
- Writing with a pen makes you think; handwritten notes are special.
- Think about what you want to say before you start.

These three basic skills—listening, speaking, and writing—are fundamental to your long-term success. Tony Robbins, writing in *Unlimited Power*, characterized their value this way:

The way we communicate with others and with ourselves ultimately determines the quality of our lives.

Something to think about ... and possibly some important choices to make too.

Section 7
Conducting Yourself Properly

PERSONAL NOTES AND REMINDERS

*The
choices
we make today
will define our lives
tomorrow.*

8

IMPROVING
YOUR COUNTRY

We tend to take our life in America and the freedoms we enjoy for granted. We seldom stop and think that we are very lucky to be living here. But things can change, and there is no guarantee that what has been accomplished in this country in the past will continue into the future. In fact, some are concerned that many important things are changing already ... unfortunately, not for the better. This seems to be a good time to take stock of the choices you and I are making that might lead to improvements in the communities in which we live and in our country as a whole.

CHOICES ADDRESSED IN THIS SECTION

The Choice to

Make Things Better
Use Your Freedom of Speech in a Positive Way
Work Together and Achieve Together
Do Your Part
Put Your Freedom to Good Use

The Choice to
Make Things Better

In spite of instant communications and the ability to be in touch with almost anyone at any time, we seem to be growing apart in this country. Instead of working and pulling together to make this a better place for everyone, there seem to be more differences, more destructive talk, and an increasing number of people more interested in being right in their position than in making this country a better place for everyone. President Abraham Lincoln, speaking many years ago, warned us of this condition:

America will never be destroyed from the outside.
If we falter and lose our freedoms,
it will be because we destroyed ourselves.

What are you and I going to do about these circumstances? Are we going to sit by and, in effect, become a part of the problem ourselves? Are we going to be indifferent about the differences that seem to become greater each day? Are we going to just leave it to others to find a better way? Or are we going to use our hearts and heads—instead of our emotions—and help make this country a better place? Clearly, it's a very important choice that you and I need to make.

But how do we make things better?

By viewing people as individuals.
We have to stop assessing a person's character based on group stereotypes such as black, white, Mexican, Muslim, Democrat, Republican, or even police. Instead, we should see each other as individuals ... as fathers, mothers, and children; as brothers and sisters; as men and women with hopes, dreams, and aspirations of doing something worthwhile with our lives. Fathers wanting to provide for their families, mothers wanting to create warm and happy homes, children wanting to learn and be successful ... the vast majority of us are good people trying to do good things and have a happy

life. We have to recognize we share this common goal of pursuing happiness, and start working closer together to achieve exactly that for everyone.

By doing something to improve the community in which you live.
According to the United States Bureau of Labor Statistics, only about 25 percent of us volunteer to help others in some way. And this percentage has remained relatively flat over the past twelve years. So ask yourself: Which group do I fall into, the 25 percent who *do*, or the 75 percent who *don't*? If it's the latter, maybe it's time for you to join in, get to work, and become a part of the solution.

By being less critical.
Many of us were taught, "Let him who is without sin cast the first stone." But today, many of us pay almost no attention to what we're doing wrong or what's wrong in our own lives as we shout out or protest against others. Being openly critical of others never made anything better. It takes caring people, working quietly but always diligently, to make our communities better places to live.

America will never be a perfect place. But working together we can make it much better than it is today. We can forget about labels and look at people as individuals. We can stop making broad assumptions and recognize that most people are good folks, wanting a happy life. We can share the love reflected by God's spirit in us and make others feel that someone truly cares about them. Ralph Waldo Emerson, writing in one of his many essays, explained our purpose this way:

The purpose of life is not to be happy.
It is to be useful, to be honorable, to be compassionate,
to have it make some difference that you have lived.

Make the choice to make a difference, to work to make things better.

Then get up and go do it.

The Choice to
Use Your Freedom of Speech in a Positive Way

Does our freedom of speech give us the right to say anything about anybody? While legally speaking it usually does, that *definitely* does not mean we should! Free speech gives us every right to say what we want, but we should not use our words to hurt others. There is a constructive way and a destructive way to say what's on our mind ... a positive way and a negative way to express our opinion ... even a helpful way and a hurtful way to be critical of others. It's important that we understand the difference.

The power of free speech is a timely subject. We're being barraged with defamatory words these days. It's very easy to take "potshots" on the internet, and more and more people are doing so. Politicians are on the news not just attacking someone's ideas, but also criticizing and demeaning those whose opinions differ from theirs. And most television interviews these days contain loaded questions intended more to be a "gotcha" moment than to obtain information on a matter of real importance. You have to be careful not to let all this negativity bring out the negativity in you. Just because more and more people are being negative about things doesn't make it the right thing for you and me to do.

Our words can do a lot of damage. For example, a university was recently in the news after fraternity members there made racist remarks. The remarks were recorded and sent to the president of the school. He took prompt action by closing the fraternity, ordering members to vacate their fraternity house by midnight, and expelling several of them. It was just a few words, but those words caused damage not only to black students on that campus but to students and others around the country as well.

This little statement is something we should all keep in mind: "If you don't have something nice to say, just don't say anything at all." If those young fraternity members had made better choices about their words—or, better yet, said nothing at all—people would not have been hurt, and a very troublesome event would have been avoided.

This Arabian proverb reminds us of the benefit of controlling what we say:

When you have spoken the word, it reigns over you.
When it is unspoken, you reign over it.

So what should we keep in mind as we work to use our freedom of speech in a positive way?

Never use words to intentionally hurt others.
Learn to keep your wits about you, always be respectful of others, and use the English language in an intelligent way to make your point.

Have the facts.
Everyone has the right to his or her opinion, but fewer and fewer of the ones we hear these days are actually based on facts. Remember, the more your opinion is based on fact, the more likely you are to have a correct one.

Address the issue, not the person.
We have many issues in this country that need to be addressed, but we should explain our views without demeaning those who see things differently.

Practice saying more good and positive things.
To break from the influence of the critical comments we hear, go out of your way to say something nice to many of the people you see each day. A French king reminded us centuries ago of who we become when we do otherwise:

If a civil word or two will render a person happy,
he must be a wretch indeed who will not tell them to him.

Words have power. They can make people happy, sad, or mad. They can cause people to respect you or walk away in dismay. Make the choice to use your freedom of speech wisely. Work to improve lives with your words, never to hurt someone with them. It's an important choice for all of us to make.

The Choice to
Work Together and Achieve Together

With so many different backgrounds, beliefs, and opinions, how could anyone in their right mind ever expect people to actually work together and achieve together? It seems to be an impossible expectation and a waste of time to even entertain such a thought. We see the title above, but quickly think, "That's a nice objective, but it's impossible to achieve."

Granted, we're never going to blow a whistle and have everyone in this country start working together in a cooperative way. But you and I don't have to wait for everyone else to change. We can promote working together and achieving together in our own sphere of influence … within our families and within the communities in which we live. We can make a special effort, even when the project is small and the people few in number, to work in a helpful and cooperative way.

Never doubt that a small group of thoughtful, committed citizens can change the world. Indeed, it is the only thing that ever has.

Margaret Meade, Cultural Anthropologist

As you reflect on working and achieving with others, here are three choices to consider:

Treat others and their ideas with respect.
This includes those with whom you disagree, even those who may be outspoken in exposing their views and opinions. It takes a smart, classy, good person to show respect, especially when ideas different from theirs are being discussed. You can be the person who sets the example for showing respect for others and the ideas they have.

Become committed to the group's success.
Individual ideas and efforts are fundamental to any group's success. However, when working in a group with others—whether it's your neighborhood committee or a team of associates at work—you should switch your objective from pushing your own personal

122

opinion to developing the collective thinking of the group. In other words, the goal is not about what you want to do but what the group, ultimately, is able to achieve together.

Work to develop understanding within the group.
Most issues of importance today are complicated, seldom fully understood at first blush. When the topic is important, help the group to do its research, review facts, consider alternatives, and develop a solid understanding about the issue at hand.

It was in a southern state. The Confederate flag had flown directly under the American flag for over sixty years. And many citizens thought it should remain that way. But two freshmen state senators had just been sworn in, and each wanted to "make his mark" while working to make the state a better place to live. Bob was white and his family had lived prominently in the state for over one hundred years. Earl was an African American, his family had struggled most of his life, and he was the first to get a college degree. Jobs, budgets, and healthcare were high on both of their agendas. Bob had his marching orders from home to "leave the flag where it is," and Earl had long felt the need to change things. Instead of waiting for the senate to get into full swing, Bob approached Earl to congratulate him on his election, but more specifically to ask him to dinner to determine how they might best work together. Over that dinner, Bob came to understand how Earl and his friends felt when they saw that flag flying over the capitol every day. Committing to work together on a solution, they soon introduced a joint bill (the Single Flag Bill, as it was called) and both spoke emotionally in its support. It passed 47–3. It will be very interesting to see what these two accomplish as they work together and achieve together in the years to come. My bet is ... they will accomplish a lot.

Through your actions and demeanor, you can encourage others to work together and achieve together. You can be a noticeable example of a careful thinker, someone who shows respect for everyone, and who clearly wants to work to develop effective ideas and solutions that are good for all. Working together is an important sport. We need more citizens—and more politicians—who understand this.

The Choice to
Do Your Part

On a recent trip to Washington, DC, I stood in front of the flag that flew over Fort McHenry during the Battle of Baltimore with the British in the War of 1812. I went on from there and toured the American History portions of the Smithsonian, viewing images of all the wars in which brave men and women fought for this country. More than 1.1 million Americans have given their lives in wars to protect our country and preserve the freedoms you and I enjoy today. These men and women gave their lives for us. They gave us the freedom to make the choices we make today. Therefore, it seems fair to ask: "What are you and I doing to honor the freedom these men and women fought to provide?"

Almost all of us take our life in America and the freedoms we enjoy for granted. We don't view the preservation and continued improvement of America as a personal responsibility. We leave that job to others. Nevertheless, we're very quick to criticize when we think something is wrong. Lots of talkers about problems here, but little action to help fix them. Unfortunately, that applies to many of us.

It is easy to take liberty for granted,
when you have never had it taken from you.

Attributed to M. Grundler

Let's stop and think about this: What can you and I do to protect our country and make it an even better place for everyone? Here are four choices you can consider making:

Make the choice to expand your knowledge of America.
We can't appreciate the freedom we have today if we don't understand the work and sacrifices that others have made on our behalf. Almost all of us need to know more about America's history, our hard-fought wars, and how the country functions today. To update your basic understanding of America's history, do some homework. There are dozens of well-developed websites that can help you become more informed about America.

124

Make the choice to actively engage with your politicians.

As this is being written, our national debt is approaching $20 trillion, and our towns and cities are struggling to pay for basic services. While these financial problems grow worse, politicians, who have performed poorly for many years, continue to argue with each other while failing to develop real solutions to our problems. Don't just wait to vote; get actively involved now and let your elected officials know specifically what should be done.

Make the choice to support the individuals who protect us.

There are over 1.3 million men and women in the United States armed services (plus 1 million in the reserves) protecting American interests throughout the world. In addition, there are over 1 million local police officers, FBI personnel, and other agents who work each day to intercept growing threats here at home. In our own individual ways, we need to reach out and show our appreciation to these individuals who put their lives on the line for us ... every day.

Make the choice to get more involved in your local community.

Freedom of speech was fundamentally important in the development of our country. So speak up and get involved in an issue or project that needs to be addressed. We must protect our freedom of speech, and those of us who really care about this country must make sure it is exercised in an honest, truthful, and helpful way.

I'm concerned about people who don't appreciate our country's history. I'm concerned about people who are enjoying life in this country, but doing little or nothing to make it better. I'm concerned about people who are making choices that are hurting others and chipping away at the foundation of this great land. You'll have to decide if any of this concern applies to you.

Now is a good time to ask yourself this question: What am I doing to make my community—and this country—a better place? And what was your answer?

The Choice to
Put Your Freedom to Good Use

As mentioned previously, many of us take our freedom for granted. We get up every morning and go about our business, without stopping to think about the freedom we enjoy or to give thanks for it. Worse, some of us abuse our freedom by using it to say or do things that hurt others. Freedom is a wonderful circumstance that provides those who live under it with many opportunities. But it's the choices we make under the banner of freedom that determine how worthwhile that freedom will be.

An important question for you:
Are you putting your freedom to good use?

As you consider your answer, pause and think about the millions of people around the world who have virtually no freedom at all. Over 11 million Syrian refugees have been driven from their homeland due to war and oppression and are wondering if they will ever find a home again. There are over 5 million people in South Sudan who can't even think about freedom because they have so little to eat. Over 1.5 million are displaced in Iraq because of the senseless conflicts going on there. And, there are millions of others—here and abroad—whose freedom is being infringed upon in some way.

Therefore, those of us who are truly free should place a high value on the condition. We should consider carefully how we are using our freedom and if we are we putting it to good use. Here are three questions whose answers will help you determine if you are using your freedom in positive ways:

Are you helping others?
There are people right around you whose freedom is hampered in some way. Maybe they need financial support. Maybe they need someone to help them find a job. Maybe they need a better place to live. Maybe they need help in accomplishing some goal they have for their life. How much time are you devoting to helping someone in need?

Are you broadening your knowledge and expanding your understanding?

To be free to think is great, but the benefits of that freedom can be limited if we don't have the knowledge or understanding to take advantage of it. With so much information coming our way, we have to make the choice to reach beyond tweets and texts to read important books, research pertinent topics, take online courses, and review other materials that provide us with an informed view of the world and the events taking place within it.

Wrote my way out of the hood.
Thought my way out of poverty!
Don't tell me that knowledge isn't power.
Education changes everything.

Brandi L. Bates, Author of *Amid the Cacophony of Cries*

Are you working to do something special with your life?

As expressed many times in this book, it is my belief that our lives have an intended purpose and that our interests, motivations, and the needs of others point us to it. We have to make an assessment of ourselves to determine if we are using our freedom to identify that purpose and make it a reality within our lives. Richelle E. Goodrich, writing in *Making Wishes*, explained that freedom gives us this choice:

You are here to make a difference,
to either improve the world or worsen it.
And whether or not you consciously choose to,
you will accomplish one or the other.

So be sure you are using your freedom wisely … by helping others, by increasing your knowledge and understanding, and by working identify the intended purpose of your life. It's freedom that provides you with the opportunity to do these things. Don't waste the opportunities that freedom provides.

Section 8
Improving Your Country

PERSONAL NOTES AND REMINDERS

The
choices
we make today
will define our lives
tomorrow.

9

RESPECTING OTHERS
AS INDIVIDUALS

One of our more difficult choices is to refrain from forming an opinion of someone based on their appearance, religious beliefs, or political preferences, but to view them as a unique individual instead. Unfortunately, we have become conditioned to judge people on these three things. This, to me, is a poor choice because it hinders us, even prevents us, from really getting to know people including who they are, what they believe, and what they are trying to achieve with their lives.

Even worse, at times our shallow assessments go too far and hateful feelings emerge. "His politics are so different from mine. I just don't care to be around him." Have you ever heard someone say something similar to that? The point I'm making in this section is this: absolutely no good ever comes from our failure to respect someone as an individual. It's only when we do so and conduct ourselves in a proper way that we have opportunities to learn and gain a better understanding of the individual before us.

Most of us want the same basic things … to live in peace, to pursue our personal interests, and to feel the love of those around us. But in spite of these common objectives, too often we focus on our differences. This is something we all need to stop and think about.

CHOICES ADDRESSED IN THIS SECTION

The Choice to

Move Beyond Your First Impression
Eliminate Hate in Your Life
Recognize We Have Common Goals
Respect Our Differences
See Others as Individuals

The Choice to
Move Beyond Your First Impression

When we encounter another individual for the first time, our initial assessment is all about how they look. Are they average looking or attractive? Are they dressed well or sloppy? Are they medium size, trim, or overweight? Tall or short? Well-groomed or unkempt? Red, yellow, black, or white? All of these external views come into play in creating what we refer to as that all-important first impression.

The problem with first impressions, however, is that we let them carry more weight than they deserve. We make the mistake of deciding who this person is based on a very limited amount of information. Especially if they are attractive, we will go so far as to determine that we like them just based on what we see. Granted, these quick evaluations happen naturally and without much effort, but that doesn't mean we should accept them. Instead, you can make a different choice … you can remind yourself, right then and there, not to make an assessment of this person until you gather more information … until you know enough to determine who this person really is and what they are all about. Brad Pitt warned us of this mistake and gave us this logic for waiting until we know more before forming an opinion about someone:

> *When you see a person, do you concentrate on their looks?*
> *It's just a first impression. Then there's someone who doesn't*
> *catch your eye immediately, but you talk to them and*
> *they become the most beautiful person in the world.*

You and I need to stop to think about this. Are we allowing our opinions of others to be shaped too much by first impressions? We need to remind ourselves that, in reality, non-visual character traits are much more important in determining who a person really is, and it takes longer to understand those things about someone. In other words, we need to make the choice to wait until we know more about a person before we determine who they are. American author and poet Richelle E. Goodrich explained it this way:

I am not what you see.
I am what time and effort and interaction slowly unveil.

There are lots of opening points or questions that can help us get to know someone, including where they are from, where they went to school, what type of work they do, what family activities they enjoy, and so forth. As we hear responses and dialogue with someone, other questions will develop. As the conversation moves along, we can determine, Are they nice? Do they communicate well? Are they intelligent? Are they reaching out to help others? and much more. None of these has anything to do with how the person looks, but each piece of information provides an insight into who this person really is. As British statesman Lord Chesterfield advised us:

You must look into people,
as well as at them.

In addition to maintaining control over the influence of our first impressions, we need to learn how to evaluate people based on their character. Are they honest in their dealings with others and how they live their life? Are they kind and respectful toward those around them? Are they using their life in some way to improve the lives of others? Are they knowledgeable and reasonably informed? It takes time, good questions, and meaningful conversations to determine these things ... so don't be "trigger happy" in forming your opinion of another individual.

Until you know more about someone, don't make the poor choice of deciding who they are and whether you will like them. As Ms. Goodrich pointed out, it takes time, effort, and interaction to unveil the real person. The more effective you are in doing this, the better the group of friends and acquaintances you will have, and the less you will be fooled by someone who only looks the part.

The Choice to
Eliminate Hate in Your Life

Things get difficult sometimes. Within families, business, and school life, disagreements arise. Before you know it someone gets angry and starts saying bad things about the other person, and hateful feelings arise. Such feelings can escalate into shouting matches, and people can get hurt emotionally, even physically. When hate replaces love, anything can happen.

You and I may never get into a physical fight. But we can attack someone with our words and "swing at them" verbally. Even when we don't reveal such emotions, we can develop a strong feeling of dislike—even hate—within us. But hate accomplishes absolutely nothing. Hate only hurts us when we let it take control. Hate is like a gun that shoots its bullets backward.

Yes, hate has been in the world for thousands of years. There are groups of people who hate each other because of differences that have existed for generations. But no good has ever come from this hate. Instead, millions of lives have been lost or ruined because of it. Such actions show how destructive hate can be. People who can't make the choice to overcome their hateful feelings and replace them with something better miss the entire point of what living is all about.

Granted, we are talking about a more localized version of hate here … one that pops up between ourselves and someone around us. But like the generational hate referenced above, our hate can wipe out our opportunity to understand the other person and their point of view. It can hinder the development of a relationship and make it impossible to accomplish something meaningful together.

So how do we tone down hateful feelings when we feel them coming on? Here are three points to keep in mind—hopefully, always remember—as you work to eliminate hate from being a part of your life:

Remember, there is some good in almost everyone.
Although this good may get overshadowed at times by poorly chosen words or actions, you and I can still make the choice to

look for the good in others. We can be less judgmental, show more respect as difficult as it might be, and remember that there is some good in almost everyone. We have to live our lives acknowledging and believing what former President Ronald Reagan explained to us with these words:

> I know in my heart that man is good,
> that what is right will always eventually triumph,
> and there is purpose and worth in each and every life.

Remember, you can always take the first step to diffuse a situation.
Sometimes we have to take a leadership role to resolve a difficult situation … even when you know you are right and the other person is wrong. Reaching out to someone and simply saying, "I'm sorry for the disagreement" can often diffuse a difficult situation. In other words, you can be the good guy if you choose to be.

Remember, you will never improve anything or anyone through hate.
When hate wins, everyone loses. When we hate, we hurt ourselves as well as others. It's impossible to use hate to make anything better. Only genuine care and concern can accomplish that. As Dr. Martin Luther King, Jr., the leader of peaceful protest, reminded us:

> Darkness cannot drive out darkness; only light can do that.
> Hate cannot drive out hate; only love can do that.

So make the choice to control yourself when you feel hate arising inside you. Make the choice to be a caring and concerned person in your dealings with others. This can be a difficult choice to make at times. But you will have a much better life—and so will those around you—if you control your hate whenever you feel it entering the scene. Once again, it's a choice only you can make.

The Choice to
Recognize We Have Common Goals

There is no magic potion that will make people care more about each other. But it's time we quit letting our differences control our actions and, instead, focus on what we have in common. Almost everyone in this world wants exactly the same things—to live in peace, to take care of our families, to pursue work and activities we want to do, and to feel the love of those around us. Red, yellow, black, or white … east, west, north, or south—whatever our background or circumstances—almost all of us want the same things.

Though we cannot think alike, may we not love alike?
May we not be of one heart, though we are not of one opinion?
Without all doubt, we may.

John Wesley, Founder of the Methodist Church

The point is this—we are much more alike than we are different. We need to put our differences aside and celebrate our similarities, ultimately showing more love and care for one another. Never has there been a greater need for people everywhere in this world to "put down their swords" and work together to make this a safer and better planet for everyone. Make no mistake, if we are to improve these circumstances, it must start with you and me and the choices we are willing to make. So, you quickly ask, What can I possibly do to improve things?

It's an important question, so let's clarify a few things. I'm not asking you to go out and change the world, but rather to start a "we're more alike than different" movement within yourself and in your daily interaction with others. I'm not asking you to go out and make speeches, but rather to live your life as a kind and caring individual who is an example for others to follow. I'm not asking you to donate money, but rather to give your time to help those who have been targets of ill feelings, even hate. Within an overall effort to develop more love and caring in this world, there is an important role for you and me. To fulfill this role, there are three basic qualities we need to practice:

Acceptance.

You and I should exhibit a greater level of acceptance toward others, especially when they look, believe, or act differently. In spite of external differences, our hearts are virtually the same and we all want the same thing … to find peace, love, and happiness for ourselves and our families.

Understanding.

We should remind ourselves of the need to get to know people as individuals and to try to understand more—including their background, goals, and needs—before we let ill feelings creep into our hearts due to a lack of personal knowledge about them.

Goodness.

It is through our choices that we bring goodness into greater focus and increase its presence within our lives. By sharing this goodness with others and caring about them as individuals, you and I, in our own special way, can help others have better lives, thus making the world a better place.

*To realize that all people are alike
and all are different is the beginning of wisdom.*

Jeffrey Fry, *Distilled Thoughts*

Stop and think about this quote for a few minutes … we are all *alike* and we are all *different*. It is this insight that can help us greatly as we interact with others each day. It is this insight that can help us understand that we are unique individuals, but wanting to achieve much the same things. It is this insight that can help us develop deeper and more meaningful relationships. It is this insight that can help us live a more productive and congenial life.

May God's spirit help us to be more loving toward one another, and to understand: we are all alike and all are different. What a valuable insight to have and live by.

The Choice to
Respect Our Differences

Why do we expect other people to think like us? Or to believe like us? Or even to look like us? Why don't we have more respect for the differences between ourselves and those around us? Showing respect for others is a choice. This choice can significantly improve our ability to communicate with others. It can increase the opportunities we have to learn and grow as human beings. And the bonus for respecting differences? We develop friendships and relationships that we would not have otherwise had.

When it comes to respecting differences, here are three points that you and I should remember:

Showing respect doesn't mean that you automatically like someone or agree with them.

Instead, it shows that you have elected to take the high road and to conduct yourself in a proper or professional way regardless of any perceived differences that may exist.

By choosing to be respectful, you create the opportunity for an understanding to develop.

We know from our life experiences that the truth often lies somewhere in between opposing views. Being respectful gives you the chance to learn and come to understand other points of view.

You could be the one who is "different."

We could be wrong in fact or attitude. We could be the one who is actually being different. Being respectful gives you the time to really understand what's going on and to determine if your outlook or opinion is correct … or not.

> We must live together as brothers,
> or perish together as fools.
>
> Dr. Martin Luther King, Jr.

There is one other point we should keep in mind here ... it's the role that self-discipline plays when differences become apparent to us. Respecting differences between ourselves and others is dependent on our ability to be self-disciplined. If you're weak when it comes to this personal quality, the more likely you are to become opinionated, sometimes very quickly, about the differences you see or experience with another individual. In other words, it's a lack of self-control that allows our lack of respect to develop ... especially when we don't really know the other individual. This is not an easy choice to make, but we should work to have control over ourselves and get to know someone better before we allow ourselves to become disrespectful, whether silently within ourselves or openly in front of others.

A flippant, frivolous man may ridicule others,
may controvert them, scorn them;
but he who has any respect for himself seems to have
renounced the right of thinking meanly of others.

Johann Wolfgang von Goethe

The choice to be respectful of others will make a big difference in your life. Learning to conduct yourself in a respectful way is, in effect, learning how to view other individuals. You and I need to understand that we need to "see" others with more than just our eyes. Doe Zantamata, author of *Happiness in Your Life*, reminded us of the importance of viewing others in a broader way with these words:

When I see you through my eyes, I think we are different.
When I see you through my heart, I know we are the same.

Differences exist ... different skills, beliefs, education levels, goals, interests, backgrounds, looks, attitudes, and more. But we shouldn't let differences divide us. Why? Because we have a lot of work left to do to fix this world and make it a good and safe place for everyone. We'll only get that job done by showing respect for each other and working together for the good of all.

The Choice to
See Others as Individuals

More than ever, we identify people as members of various groups. Ethnic groups—white, black, Mexican, and so forth; religious groups—Catholic, Baptist, Muslim, Mormon, and many more; and, of course, political groups—typically Democrat, Republican, or Independent. Participation in these groups shapes our thinking and, to some extent, defines who we are.

I'm not saying that our group memberships aren't important. Each of these groups contributes to life in our communities and in the world in some special way. Our differences provide us with opportunities to learn from each other and to understand other views of life. But we have a real need to put group designations aside and think of each other as individuals … people with hearts, minds, and souls who want to be happy and accomplish something important with their lives.

Without taking the time to get to know someone on an individual basis, we tend to see them as a group member and consider them to be much the same as others in that group. However, when we make the effort to get to know them, we find an individual with hopes, dreams, and even problems much like our very own.

We should remind ourselves that we are here to help each other achieve more in life. Individuals with different experiences, beliefs, skills, and needs create a "real world" in which we have the opportunity to learn, grow, and live a life that helps others in some special way. The importance of connecting on an individual level was a focus of singer-songwriter John Denver, who said this:

> I believe that we are here for each other. Everything comes from an understanding that you are a gift in my life —whoever you are, whatever our differences.

Granted, there are some bad apples in every group … a small percentage whose actions can spoil our attitude toward the group as a whole. However, we must guard against group thinking and here is why. Because almost all the people in "that group" are good people who want to find love, happiness, and contentment in life … just like you and me.

No question, there are forces that cause us to be group thinkers. We dislike groups whose members have failed to understand that the purpose of life is to help others, not to hurt them. And we encounter special-cause groups taking positions with which we disagree. These are real-world circumstances that may justify some group thinking on our part, but that in no way excuses us from being kind and considerate when we encounter people on an individual basis.

José had moved to town from Mexico during the summer with his parents who had immigrated legally with plans to become U.S. citizens. José was twelve years old and was working hard to improve his English. His parents enrolled him in the sixth grade in the local school and, while he had been excited about his new future, his first two weeks at school were anything but enjoyable. Few of the kids made any effort to say hello, much less welcome him to the school. In addition to the stares he encountered, he overheard someone say, "He needs to go back to where he came from." Ben Alexander picked up on what was happening and made the choice to do something about it. He not only introduced himself to José, but he became José's "school guide," showing him around, answering his questions, and even inviting him over to his house after school. When other students saw what Ben was doing, they started doing things to help José feel more welcomed as well. As things worked out, José had a successful first year, became a starter on the soccer team, and made lots of new friends. However, without the choice that Ben made at the beginning of the year, things might have worked out very differently.

Let's work harder at being here for each other and view those around us as gifts in our lives, individuals with whom we can work to accomplish good things for everyone. Most of us want to do our part to make the world a better place. Let's make the choices that will allow that to happen.

Section 9
Respecting Others as Individuals

PERSONAL NOTES AND REMINDERS

*The
choices
we make today
will define our lives
tomorrow.*

10

GETTING THROUGH DIFFICULT TIMES

Everyone encounters difficult and challenging times in life. No one is immune from those "down and out" feelings when we think the world is working against us. This section reminds us that at times like these our choices take on added importance. We can choose our way out of difficult circumstances if we are willing to make new, but most likely very difficult, choices. Wishing and hoping things will change will do us little or no good. If we want to move to a better place, we have to be willing to make the choices that will take us there.

CHOICES ADDRESSED IN THIS SECTION

The Choice to

Learn from Our Mistakes
Work Your Way Out
Rebuild Hope
Change
Choose a New Life

The Choice to
Learn From Our Mistakes

Everyone makes mistakes. Sometimes it's because we weren't smart with our choice ... we knew we shouldn't have done something, but we did it anyway. Sometimes our desires overpower our common sense ... we didn't stop to think about the situation and messed up in a big way. At other times, we simply followed the crowd only to find out later that the crowd had no idea what they were doing. Mistakes come in all shapes and sizes, and everyone makes their share of them.

Because we can learn so much from our mistakes, we need to give the category of *making mistakes* some careful thought as we work to make better choices in our lives. Our goal should be to never make a mistake, but that's just not realistic. The smart person is not one who never makes mistakes, but one who knows what to do when a mistake has been made. So, the important question is this: What choices should you make when you know you've made a significant mistake?

Accept complete responsibility for your mistake.
Never blame your mistakes on someone else. The only way you can position yourself for learning and improvement is to accept that it was *your* miscue, *your* error, *your* choice, *your* mistake. If you are going to get the full benefit of learning from your mistake, the process starts by accepting full responsibility for it.

> *More people would learn from their mistakes*
> *if they weren't so busy denying that they made them.*
>
> Anonymous

Apologize to those involved.
Some level of repentance is always required to get on the other side of a mistake. If you have wronged or hurt others in some way, you must apologize ... and the sooner the better. A face-to-face

146

apology is by far the best. But a phone call, an email, or a handwritten note can suffice if distance is a factor. If your mistake didn't involve others, then it's time for you to go look in the mirror and apologize to yourself for wasting part of your life in such a way.

Identify and confirm what you will change.

So that you can grow and improve as a result of your mistake, you have to be specific about what or how you will change in the future. This is not a generalized, "Well, I'm going to try to be a better person." It has to be much more specific, such as, "I will never say something like that about Mary again." You have to be specific about the change you will make if you want to benefit from the mistake you have made. Any effort to generalize about the circumstances is a "skip-over" with no benefit derived.

Focus on making better choices in all areas of your life.

If you made a bad choice in one area, there's a good chance you are making some poor choices in other areas of your life as well. So, consider a big mistake to be the tip of the iceberg and take the time to look below the surface to determine how effective you are in making choices in other areas of your life. Maybe there are other things you need to change before more mistakes appear.

Learning from our mistakes is not a normal or natural process. We don't like to admit that we've made a mistake or have done something wrong, so we work to mentally cover it up and, in effect, hide it from ourselves. However, as I have pointed out in this book, living a meaningful and worthwhile life depends, first and foremost, on being an honest person ... with ourselves and with others. If you and I are ever going to learn from our mistakes, we must be willing to be honest about them.

Experience is not what happens to a man.
It is what a man does with what happens to him.

Aldous Huxley, *Text and Pretexts*

147

The Choice to
Work Your Way Out

We've all experienced tough times when we felt like life just wasn't working for us. Maybe it was one significant thing that caused it … a big problem at work or at school, a major disagreement with a friend or family member, or the sudden realization that our financial resources weren't going to be enough. Or it could have been a combination of things. Life just piled up on us, and we're not only feeling down about our circumstances, we're actually a little depressed about them too. Whatever their cause, every one of us experiences feelings like these at various times during our lives. The important question is: What can we do to eliminate them and feel better about things?

Work, not wish.

First, let's agree on one fundamental point. You're going to have to *work* your way out of such feelings or circumstances. *Wishing* that things would change is okay, but it's not likely to do very much. *Waiting* for things to change is not a practical strategy unless you're recovering from an illness or accident. *Praying* may help you gain insight into adjustments you need to make, but prayer alone won't reverse your course. Only *work* supported by productive choices—specific things that you actually do—can right your ship and get you headed in a better direction. Former President Barack Obama gave us some very good advice in this regard:

The best way to not feel hopeless is to get up and do something.
Don't wait for good things to happen to you.

Identify needed choices and make them.

If you agree that you're going to have to do something to get back on top of things, the question that pops up is this: What specific things can I do to change my situation and the way I feel? Here's where those all-important choices come back into the picture. You're going to have to give some careful and honest thought to the choices you need to make. You're going to have to look inside yourself, think about your past choices that created this difficulty, and identify the choices that your life is calling for now. There's a saying by an unknown author titled "Choices, Chances, Changes" that summarizes this advice quite well:

You must make a CHOICE to take a CHANCE,
or your life will never CHANGE.

Adjust your focus from yourself to others.
We could end this topic here because everyone is different, in different circumstances and in need of making different kinds of choices. Such choices could be concerned with career, relationships, finances, or many other areas of life. So, I leave the specific choices you need to make to you. However, in circumstances like these, when almost all of our time is being devoted to worrying about ourselves, it is important to be reminded that the basic purpose of our lives is to help others, not ourselves. So, as you consider other adjustments in your life, be sure to consider your answers to this very important question: What am I doing to help another individual have a better life?

Those who are happiest are those who do the most for others.
Booker T. Washington, *Up from Slavery*

There are other important choices you will need to make. But this last one may be the most important of all. Focusing your life on helping someone will add lift and meaning to your own life. As I have stated previously, if there is a secret to a fulfilling life, it has to have something to do with how we use our lives to make another person's life better. So when you include how your life will help others in the choices you make, you're almost guaranteed to move from feeling down to feeling that your life has meaning and purpose. That's just how life works ... helping "the other guy" is the key.

The Choice to
Rebuild Hope

Troubles and problems seem to be almost everywhere.

In the world ... wars have driven millions of men, women, and children from their homes. Terrorists kill innocent civilians for no reason at all. And nuclear threats continue to come from many countries.

Here at home ... shootings and killings in many cities are at all-time highs. There are increasing confrontations with policemen. And politicians have become more adept at verbal attacks than in actually solving problems for the people.

And in our personal lives ... financial pressures, relationships that aren't working well, lack of good-paying jobs, family members who have become disappointments ... these and other difficulties make us worry at times about the real benefit of life and living.

How can we possibly have hope for the future with all of these bad things taking place? This may be one of the most difficult questions you and I will ever try to answer. In fact, it would be much easier to ignore the question altogether. But we can almost be guaranteed that we will never feel better if we take a just-don't-think-about-it approach to life. There are things you and I can do. As unbelievable as it may seem right now, you and I can make a difference. Former First Lady Michelle Obama gave us this insight about being active in the pursuit of hope:

You may not always have a comfortable life.
And you will not always be able to solve all of the world's problems
at once. But don't ever underestimate the impact you can have,
because history has shown us that courage can be contagious,
and hope can take on a life of its own.

So what can we do to bolster our hope for the future?

In the world ... join and become active in a global or national cause.
Granted, some problems are so far away it's much easier to just overlook them. But those hungry children, those war-torn families, those people who lost their homes in the hurricane ... all individuals who need someone to care about them. As strange as it may seem, regaining our hope starts with helping someone in need regain theirs. Start your hope-building project by finding a group or organization that is working to make things better for others, and do your part, large or small, to help right some wrong in this world.

Here at home ... do something to help someone close by.
If there is one thing that makes us feel better, it's to reach out and help someone right around us in some way. It doesn't have to be anything major, but there are those around you, in your town or community, who are hurting in some way or need some type of assistance. Helping them will—no doubt about it—help you as well.

In your personal life ... prioritize your challenges and address them one at a time.
No matter who you are, there will always be problems to overcome. The key is not to sit back and just worry about them, but to make specific choices to move your life in a better direction. Make a list of what you consider to be your current challenges, prioritize them in some way, and go to work on resolving one of them. Then, move on to another. You can make your life better, certainly not all at once, but definitely by making choices to resolve them ... one problem at a time.

Rebuilding hope won't happen if you just sit there. It requires you to make choices. To help people in the world whose lives have been impacted in some way, to reach out to someone close by you to improve their life, and to work to resolve that first problem on your personal list. Interestingly, two of these choices are about helping others; only one is about you. Focusing totally on yourself never rekindles hope. Helping others find hope always does.

The Choice to
Change

Are you satisfied with your life right now?
Are you pleased with the relationships you have?
Are you making a difference in the lives of others?

If your answers to these questions are yes and you're happy about the general direction of your life, "keep on trucking" as they say. If not, if there is something you want to change, this topic is for you.

As you think about how you have been living your life, what specifically would you like to change? Maybe it's something you've been doing wrong and you want to stop. Maybe it's something you've been motivated to do for some time, but never marshaled the courage to launch the effort. Maybe it's an academic or physical improvement project that you want to complete. It's your life and only you can determine what this change should be.

Once you have identified the change you want to make, thought about it, and reconfirmed it to yourself, write it down on paper or record it in your device. Take it out and look at it every day. Yes, every day. And as you review it each day, list the choices under it that you need to make for this change to become a reality. Most big accomplishments take place through a series of small choices. So keep updating your list of choices, add new ones as needed, and check off the ones you have completed. This is, in effect, your choice management report, so keep it up-to-date. You can make a major change in your life a reality if you make *managing your choices* part of your daily routine.

Wishing and hoping are nice activities, but they won't change your life. But those powerful little choices can change your life in significant ways. Coming to this realization ... that your life is managed, developed, and ultimately defined by the choices you make is the most important "life management" insight you will ever have.

Armed with that understanding, you can focus on the choices you need to make to develop your life in a more meaningful way.

John had always placed a high value on having fun and enjoying time with friends. So much so that he would tell his parents he was going somewhere to study when, in fact, he was riding around town with his two buddies, William and Shane. While they were never real trouble-makers during their high school years, they "advanced" in their ability to find activities that supported their prefer-to-party lifestyles. This ability started to pick up speed during their sophomore year, when they would meet on Friday and Saturday nights to drink beer that an older guy had purchased for them. It continued into their junior year when they started smoking pot together, sometimes even on weeknights. By their senior year, William was experimenting with a couple of drugs and Shane was well on his way to joining the opioid epidemic. At this point, William wasn't going to graduate due to his grades and Shane had dropped out of school altogether. As John sat one afternoon thinking about these circumstances and all the "fun" the three of them had had the past few years, he came to the sudden realization that all of them were wasting their lives. He wondered, even out loud to himself, how they could have been so stupid to do these things. After a long one-on-one discussion with the high school guidance counselor, Mr. Davis said to him, "John, you can make the choice to continue this craziness, or you can make the choice to change."

As you move ahead with your life, remember … *every* choice counts. The good choices move you and your life forward and on to bigger and better things. The poor or bad choices hold you back, keep you from enjoying your life, and can cause you to completely miss finding your real purpose. Whatever you need or want to change, you can change it if you are willing to make the choice to do so.

Manage your choices effectively, and your life will be effective as well.

The Choice to
Choose a New Life

When a child is born, parents and family members are almost always filled with joy and optimism. Almost every new birth is accompanied with great expectations for the child and the life he or she will live. It's not unusual to hear optimistic comments as a newborn is welcomed into the world.

But we all know our lives don't always live up to this early optimism. Reality comes into play, we encounter unexpected challenges, and things don't work out the way we and others had hoped. Some of us even reach a point where we're actually disappointed with our life and wish we had a new one. You may even be feeling this way, to some degree, as you read this book.

Well, new lives aren't available. But new thinking, new choices, and new directions certainly are. We can, in fact, make our lives better—even change them completely—by making better choices. New choices, in effect, bring new life. Oprah Winfrey explained in her magazine, *O*, how important a single choice can be in moving your life in a new direction:

Right now you are one choice away
from a new beginning, one that leads you towards
becoming the fullest human being you can be.

You can't just go with the flow if you want to develop a special life. Unfortunately, that's what many people do—go along to get along, as some of us put it. For many reasons, this approach to life never works. It lets other people have more influence over your life than you do. When that lifestyle puts us in the ditch, we suddenly realize that choosing to live that way is a big mistake. Instead, you must realize that you are special and unique, and work to determine—and choose—what is best for you.

If you need a new life, call on yourself to start making new choices. These may include a choice to do that special thing you've always wanted to do with your life. It may include a choice that allows you to be of much greater help to those around you or leads you to devote your life to a special cause or work. It may be a choice that requires you to move away and step beyond your comfort zone. Learning to use your choices to create a new life is an important step in this "new life" process.

Life's greatest achievement is the continual remaking of yourself, so that, at last, you do know how to live.

Winfred Rhoades, *The Self You Have to Live With*

And, you have to be willing to work at it. A new life doesn't come easy. You have to be willing to make an exceptional effort if you want to achieve an important result. Making these new choices is one thing; turning them into reality is another. They will require a great deal of work and perseverance on your part. But much happiness can come from making such an effort.

This may be hard to believe, especially if you have been through some really tough times, but you can choose your way out of almost any circumstances. Although you may have shut out the goodness in your life with your past choices, that goodness is still available to be amplified within you. Although you may have paid no attention to the real purpose of your life, that purpose still exists. By utilizing the power of your choices, you can expand the goodness in your life and live in a more purposeful way … in effect, creating a new life for you.

Rachel spent most afternoons cruising the internet and most evenings out cruising with her friends. But today she was in no cruising mood. She had learned she failed two courses and would not be graduating from high school with her friends. After coming to the realization that she had been wasting her academic life, she decided she would work harder and do better in the future. Will she and, as a result, start creating a new life? It all depends on the choices she is willing to make.

Section 10
Getting through Difficult Times

PERSONAL NOTES AND REMINDERS

*The
choices
we make today
will define our lives
tomorrow.*

11

THINKING WISELY

Stopping to think about your life and how you are living it is a worthwhile exercise. You've probably noted that I've mentioned the need to stop and think many times in this book. It's because we encounter so much information these days and are subject to so many influences on our lives. From time to time we need to step away from all of this, stop and think about our life, and refocus on what's good and wise for us as we work to make better choices and live in a more meaningful way.

CHOICES ADDRESSED IN THIS SECTION

The Choice to
Stop and Think
Just Let It Go
Stop Making Excuses
Stop Criticizing Others
Manage the Moments
Take Care of Your Body
Quit Pretending
Watch Out for the Train Wreck
End Up Somewhere

The Choice to
Stop and Think

When I went to work for IBM many years ago, the company gave its employees pocket-size notepads with one word printed on the cover: THINK. Referred to as "think pads," these were daily reminders to think about what you were doing and the decisions you were making, for yourself and for your customers. Obviously, that little reminder to think about things has served IBM well as it is one of the leading technology companies in the world today.

Stopping to think can be of great benefit to you and me as well. Many times we do things or make important choices without giving them the thought they deserve. When we do that, especially when the choice turns out to be a poor one, we often look back and wonder, what in the world was I thinking? So, remember to stop and think about what you are doing … to give some careful thought to the choices you are making and to how you are choosing to live your life.

There was a story recently about a high school basketball player who faced a difficult choice. His team had won the state championship the previous year, and he was selected to the all-state team. But in spite of his exceptional basketball skills, the young man wanted to be a professional dancer. He knew if he wanted to dance professionally, however, he would have to devote more time and effort to achieving that goal. After much thought and deliberation, he made the choice to give up basketball to join the school dance team … a very difficult choice in those circumstances. The article highlighted how much thought he put into his choice, including long discussions with his NFL quarterback dad; obtaining input from other family members, teammates, and coaches; and aligning his choice with his feeling inside that professional dancing was what he was intended to do. If he had not taken the time to think through his choice, he likely would have continued to be a basketball player … a very good one, but one who would have been second-guessing himself for his entire life.

Henry Ford gave us this observation about thinking:

Thinking is the hardest work there is,
which is probably the reason why so few engage in it.

Most of our choices are straightforward and require little thought to confirm the right thing for us to do. But some of our choices can be life changers as was the case with the high school basketball player. Those choices require that we make an extended effort to do our research, discuss it with people we trust, talk to ourselves about it, and, to the extent possible, determine if it syncs with our intended purpose in life. There is no set way to go about all of this, but the better and more diligent you are in completing your thinking process, the higher the quality of your choice will be.

The effectiveness of the life we ultimately live almost totally depends on how well we think and, subsequently, the choices we make. While there are physical and circumstantial differences from one person to the next, the real factor that differentiates people is how effectively they think. While external things may define us on the outside, who we really are is defined on the inside ... by what we think. James Allen, in *Above Life's Turmoil*, explained how our life rides on our thoughts:

You are today where your thoughts have brought you.
You will be tomorrow where your thoughts take you.

I have devoted this book to the objective of helping people make better choices. To do this, you have to THINK about the choices you make. Stopping to think, as mentioned many times in this book, will not only improve the choices you and I make each day, but it can make the fundamental difference between a great choice and a poor one.

Don't let poor choices define your life. Let *good thinking* do it.

The Choice to
Just Let It Go

Almost all of us have done it: that moment when you know the route you suggested was faster than the one your friend actually took. You were aching to say it, so you did. "I told you so!"

Or you cross paths with someone who thinks differently, who has an opinion opposite from your own. You can't hold back, so you speak right up, point out why you think the other person is wrong, and proceed to expound, sometimes forcefully, on your position.

But did your "correcting comments" really change anything? Didn't you and your traveling friend make it to your final destination okay? Didn't you depart that conversation with the same opinions you two had when the disagreement started? In almost all such situations, nothing really changes. Except for one thing ... we damage our relationship with the other person.

For some strange reason, we think it is okay to speak right up and point things out when we think someone is wrong. But if we stop and think about it, there's a better choice we can make. You can make the choice not to say anything ... to just let it go. You can remain silent, bite your tongue if you must, and let the moment pass. As you consider how you will conduct yourself the next time one of these "moments of difference" occurs, here are four things to keep in mind:

First, *sharp exchanges never benefit anyone* and never improve our relationships with others. That can only be accomplished through mutual respect, even when significant differences exist.

Second, *we could be the one who is wrong* or off in our thinking. We almost always believe that we are right and "they" are wrong, but that's just not the case.

Third, *we only learn when we listen.* Getting on our high horse about our view of things can diminish or even eliminate an opportunity to learn something new and grow a little bit.

Fourth, *self-discipline requires a special effort.* It's not something that just happens. We have to recognize when we need to "call on ourselves" to act in a proper and respectful way.

Newton's third law (of physics) is usually summarized this way: *for every action there is an equal and opposite reaction.* While this applies to our physical world, it seems to me that we can apply it to situations like these as well. Simply stated, although our intentions may have been good, our words can create just the opposite reaction in the one who hears them.

This is not to say that we don't have strong feelings about things we believe are not right, or that need to be changed in some way. But we should remind ourselves that quick or strong words will seldom improve anything. Instead, we should be willing to actually work at something—not just talk about it—to achieve better things for everyone.

So the next time you feel the hair popping up on the back of your neck, remember that you have choices. Yes, you can speak up sharply or write one of those gotcha texts. Or you can just let it go. You can remain silent, keep your fingers off the keyboard or your mouth shut, and let the moment pass. You can control yourself and forego the opportunity to "prove your point."

The world would be happier
if men had the same capacity to be silent
that they have to speak.

Baruch Spinoza, Dutch Philosopher

Not easy, but you can use this powerful choice to everyone's advantage ... the choice to just let it go.

The Choice to
Stop Making Excuses

Life is not fair, easy, or perfect. Life has its share of challenges, disappointments, and even outright failures. Truth be told, most of us have more reasons why our life should not be a success than reasons why it should. But one major difference between those who develop their lives effectively and those who don't is a willingness to stop making excuses, to fully acknowledge their circumstances, and to make the choices needed to turn their lives into something meaningful and worthwhile.

Offering an excuse is a refusal to accept responsibility for something. It happened or is happening, but we don't want to admit it or do the work to correct the situation. So, we offer an excuse instead. For some reason, we tend to think we will be okay if we just "explain" things. We mistakenly consider it better for our lives to blame our actions, or lack thereof, on something else. The problem this creates is twofold: first, we are not being totally honest with ourselves or others, and second, it hinders our ability to make choices that would help us improve. Benjamin Franklin, one of our country's founding fathers, described the excuse-making skill this way:

He that is good for making excuses
is seldom good for anything else.

The internal logic necessary to manage your life effectively is negated when you say one thing while knowing that the truth, or the right thing, is something quite different. You will never improve your life by making excuses or offering explanations that "justify" your actions. On the other hand, you can position yourself to make significant personal improvement if you will just be totally honest with yourself and with those around you. The ability to make better choices in your life starts with honoring the truth both on the inside and the outside of your life.

Sarah was thirty years old and at least eighty pounds overweight. Worse, she was continuing to add more weight and would probably be "a hundred over" within a year or so. In high school, she frequently responded to her mother's suggestions to exercise with replies such as, "I have to study, my grades are more important than my weight." In college, she responded to a friend who invited Sarah to join her in a special diet, "I really don't have the time to go to those group meetings." During her most recent medical checkup, she responded to the doctor's warning about health problems associated with weight by saying, "I'm going start walking this summer when the weather is better." For over fifteen years now, Sarah has been "explaining" to others why she couldn't—or wouldn't—make better health choices and lose some weight. The odds are that Sarah will have medical problems, possibly severe ones, due to her excess weight. Wonder what her excuse will be then.

Our choices, not the excuses we make, define our lives. The student who is smart but chooses to waste time and not study will produce an average to poor academic report. On the other hand, the average student who studies hard and applies himself can produce excellent results. Two people, pre-equipped for certain outcomes, so to speak, can produce opposite results due to the choices they make.

Excellence is never an accident.
It is always the result of high intention, sincere effort,
and intelligent execution; it represents the wise choice of many
alternatives — choice, not chance, determines your destiny.

Aristotle

While there may be some logic in the reason you offer for not doing a responsible thing, your life still misses the benefit of the better but more difficult choice. Those few words uttered today may get you off the hook for now, but at some point, your life will reflect the excuses you have made. The choice to never make excuses—to honor the facts instead—is a wise one indeed.

The Choice to
Stop Criticizing Others

We are often quick to criticize others but slow to be critical of ourselves. Psychologists say the practice of being critical of others helps us feel superior and allows us to avoid acknowledging our own imperfections. Whatever the reason, we will never improve our own lives—or anyone's for that matter—by criticizing or tearing down another person. Dale Carnegie, in his well-known book *How to Win Friends and Influence People*, clarified who typically criticizes others with this comment:

*Any fool can criticize, condemn, and complain —
and most fools do.*

We should be aware that we are being conditioned to be this way. We encounter social media posts and texts each day that are critical of someone, many with no basis in fact. We hear our friends taking shots at others at work or at school. Even our parents, with the best of intentions, sometimes add to our critical conditioning as they work to correct us and teach us to do the right thing. However, we should not use any of these influences as excuses for our bad conduct. We must own up to our own choices when it comes to what we say about others.

And remember this: the opportunity to talk behind someone's back—which is when most of this type of conduct occurs—does not give you or me a license to be overly critical of someone. We should remember that it's not our place or our responsibility to be openly critical of another person.

Will Howard was a hard worker. He always got to the office early and frequently stayed past five to make sure his action list was ready for the next day. He had been with the company for twelve years, moved up quickly at first, and became an assistant vice president during his seventh year. But in spite of all of his extra efforts, he seemed to be stuck at this current level. He had discussed the circumstances with his wife on several occasions, but he just didn't understand why he was being repeatedly passed over for promotion. One day the worry was getting to him, so he went to his manager's office to discuss the circumstances with him. Terry Hemphill, SVP of Operations and Will's boss for the past several years, welcomed the opportunity to discuss the topic, and decided to be very straightforward about it. "Will, you are a valued employee, there should be no question about that. But, frankly, you are far too critical of the associates below you as well as others in the company. Some of your remarks, although well intended I'm sure, actually make people feel inferior instead of motivated to do better work. As a result, we've been hesitant to put more people under you." Will sat there thinking … "I thought I was being helpful. I didn't realize my critiques were actually hindering someone's performance."

Charles Schwab, founder of the large discount brokerage firm that bears his name, gave us this helpful observation:

I have yet to find the man, however great or exalted in his station, who did not do better work and put forth greater effort under a spirit of approval than under a spirit of criticism.

You can make the choice to stop being critical of others. You can find ways to be sincerely helpful, even instructive, without being critical. If you make the choice to curtail or stop your criticism of others and start implementing that choice today, by this time next week you will feel better about yourself. Two weeks from now, even your friends and associates will start to notice. A month from now … well, that powerful little choice will be changing your life.

Clearly, not being critical of others is a choice all of us should make.

The Choice to
Manage the Moments

We have been given a life. The challenge is to live it wisely. In trying to do so, we tend to focus on the big things such as education, career, family, and money. We think seriously about these major areas of our lives and what we want to accomplish within each of them. While doing so, however, many of us overlook the small things. We fail to value the small moments we have to interact with others each day and the importance of these moments in our lives. Then one day— usually when we are older—we come to realize it's the little moments that are the fundamental ingredients in living a meaningful life, and that overlooking the importance of them is not a wise way to live.

Life is not made up
of minutes, hours, days,
weeks, months, or years,
but of moments.

Sarah Ban Breathnach, *Moving On*

Managing moments is not something we think much about. We just go about our day and, before we know it, the day is over and done … then off to bed to await another one. To become more moment-minded, it's good to establish some guidelines to help you "manage your moments" as you go about your activities each day. The following outline is a suggested set of rules or guidelines you can use, modifying as you think best, to help you manage the moments that will—collectively—define your life.

Always treat others with respect.
Your choice to treat those you encounter each day in a kind and respectful way not only will make them feel special and cared about, but you will feel value added to your life as well. Leave people feeling happy that they crossed paths with you today.

Help another person.
Through your church or a local support organization, find one person (or family) who has special needs and help them. Maybe it's a weekly bag of groceries, transportation to the clinic, or providing something specific that they need.

Volunteer.
There is strength in numbers and most nonprofit organizations need more volunteers to help carry out their work. Identify one that is doing something you believe is important and get involved. Become an active member who expands their reach.

Say thank you to those who help you.
This is such a simple thing to do, yet so surprising and meaningful to those not expecting such words from you. Just look at the store clerk who waited on you and say, "Thank you for helping me." And, note their reaction to your words.

Kiss, call, or text someone you love each day.
We take many around us for granted. We don't always feel the need to reach out to them in some way. So, make a special effort each day to kiss, call, or text someone you love or care about. Let them know they are an important part of your life.

Managing your moments may be an overly simplified concept, but it's something very important to keep in mind as we go about a typical day. Remember, you were not given your life just for your personal enjoyment, but so that, in your own unique and special ways, you could use your life to help others. The greater the degree to which you manage your moments with this objective in mind, the happier and more meaningful your life will be.

Life gives us brief moments with one another.
But sometimes in those brief moments,
we get memories that last a lifetime.

Unknown

Life is full of moments … make sure you manage them well.

The Choice to
Take Care of Your Body

According to the Centers for Disease Control and Prevention, over 65 percent of Americans are either overweight or obese. That's over two-thirds of us who are either not able or not willing to make the choices to maintain a proper weight. When you consider the correlation between being overweight and physical problems—including heart disease, high blood pressure, stroke, diabetes, and cancer—you have to wonder why people allow themselves to become this way. Some may have valid reasons, but for most of us it's a clear-cut case of outright laziness coupled with the refusal to believe that any of these health problems will ever happen "to me." There is an old saying which gives us insight about excess weight gain:

Obesity is a condition which proves that God does not help those who help themselves and help themselves and help themselves.

So, what should we be doing to improve our physical well-being? There are two basic things we can do. But before we address those, here is an important perspective we need to stop and think about. You're not in this world to live just for yourself, but to live a life that helps others in some way. If you come to accept this premise, your life takes on an added level of importance. And doing such helpful work is not always easy. We need stamina and we need to live as long as we can to fulfill our purpose and help as many people as possible. Research by The University of Oxford, as reported in the article "Obesity Takes Years Off Life Expectancy," found that moderate obesity reduces life expectancy by about three years, and severe obesity can shorten a person's life by as much as ten years.

Clearly, we should make the choices to eat properly and exercise frequently. Managing these two things is a simple, age-old health program that still works today. Because there is so much helpful information available on both of these activities (you can find plenty if you choose to search for it), I will limit my comments to two points:

There is a connection between the condition of your body and your ability to fulfill the purpose of your life.
If you can attach the benefit of eating properly and exercising regularly to fulfilling your intended purpose in life, you can develop a higher level of motivation to take proper care of yourself. Whatever your life's purpose is or turns out to be, you are not likely to live as long fulfilling it if you ignore your physical well-being.

These are everyday—not once-in-a-while—choices.
You're not going to make much progress by just jogging on Saturday morning … you have to walk/run at least two miles *every* day to achieve meaningful results. You're not going to shed many pounds just by giving up sweets … you have to eat right at *every* meal if you want to see positive results. Eating properly only a few times a week and exercising only now and then never works. You have to work at both *every* day.

Granted, you may need to start slow and increase your eating disciplines and exercise routines over time. But if you never make the choice to start, you'll never improve the condition you're in today.

We only get so much time on this earth. It just makes good sense to make choices that will help extend our stay here. Unfortunately, most of us—at least 65 percent—are either a bit lazy or refuse to recognize the correlation between healthy living and our day-to-day performance. Don't postpone the choices you need to make until it's too late. No matter what you do in life, you will do it better if you are in shape and making healthy choices every day.

*Take care of your body.
It's the only place you have to live.*
Jim Rohn, *7 Strategies for Wealth and Happiness*

The Choice to
Quit Pretending

If there is one thing that hinders our ability to make good choices the most, it must be the act of pretending. We will pretend that we can afford something and purchase it even with no idea how we will pay for it. We will pretend that we don't need to go to the doctor for a checkup, although our time to do so has already passed. We will even pretend that we are average in size when we know we're significantly overweight. Simply put, pretending is much easier than dealing with the truth.

Pretending prevents us from dealing with the facts, from assessing a situation as it really is, from accepting what needs to be done. Pretending hinders us from making precise choices that target something specific we need to improve or change. Pretending takes us out of the real world and into another where our words or actions don't reflect how things really are.

Miranda and Alex had been married for over five years and had a three-year-old daughter. Most of their friends, and even Alex for the most part, thought they were a near-perfect couple. But that was just not the case. Miranda hated when Alex left to go fishing on Saturday mornings but just couldn't bring herself to saying so since he worked so hard during the week. She didn't like the fact she and her daughter had to go to church alone when they all used to go together as a family. But when Alex explained he needed his weekend alone time, she just said, "Oh, that's okay." To make matters worse, her mother-in-law had been interfering more and more in their home life, but the last time Alex asked about it, Miranda simply said, "She means well, I'm sure." It's uncertain at this point how their marriage will work out ... clearly the odds are stacking up against it. If Miranda hadn't pretended that the Saturday fishing was acceptable, that she was okay going to church alone, that her mother-in-law's "instructions" were understandable, Alex, being the good guy he was, would have likely taken action to correct these circumstances. Without her pretending that these things were okay, Miranda would likely be feeling much better about her marriage right now.

When there is opportunity for improvement, pretending, especially when the words coming from our mouths are false, works against our ability to create a better situation and a better life. Here are a few things to think about before you enter the pretending mode again.

Pretending hurts our relationships with others.
We don't like to acknowledge that we're not always straight up with our family members and close friends. However, sooner or later, our unwillingness or inability to be honest—in a loving and caring way—hinders the depth and development of the relationship we have with others. The foundation of any relationship is truth and honesty conveyed in a respectful and proper way.

Pretending hinders understanding who we really are.
Pretending undermines who you really are and your ability to think effectively about yourself. It hinders your ability to decode the interests and motivations that can lead you to your intended purpose in life. Pretending increases the chances that you will live a life never meant for you.

Pretending impairs our ability to make good choices.
Good choices are based on facts; pretending fosters misperceptions. As a result, the more we pretend, the worse our choices are likely to be. Living in a totally honest way may make you uncomfortable at times, but it positions you to make those high-quality choices that are needed to develop and live a meaningful life.

Hell is trying to be what you are not.
Unknown

So go and pretend no more. You will be a much better person. And your life will be much better too.

The Choice to
Watch Out for the Train Wreck

We may not openly acknowledge it, but we tend to think that noth-ing really bad will ever happen to us. *I know I shouldn't be texting while driving, but I'm careful when I do it. I know I shouldn't be ex-perimenting with these drugs, but I'm only going to do it a few more times. I know I shouldn't be drinking so much with my friends, but I'm planning to cut back.* We keep doing things we know we shouldn't do, and then one day it happens. The circumstances blow up in our face and we have a "train wreck" in our life. And we immediately think, How in the world did I let this happen?

No one intends for bad things to happen. But human nature being what it is, we fool ourselves into believing that the difficult situations others face won't happen to us. I'm not sure why we think this way, but it's a clear denial of reality. For example, we knew we shouldn't, but we've always liked to drive fast. Then one day we have a major accident and several people are hurt badly.

Why do we make such choices and ignore likely outcomes? Here are the more frequent reasons we hear:

"I didn't think anything like this would ever happen to me."
Many of us just can't make ourselves accept the reality of our choices. We knew what could happen. We just refused to acknowl-edge the possibility.

"I enjoyed what I was doing and just didn't want to stop."
This one is true more often than not. We knew that we were headed for trouble, but we didn't have the guts to change or stop what we were doing.

"I intended to stop doing that but just never did."
There is a tendency to procrastinate in all of us, especially when our bad habits are involved. We knew we were doing something wrong. We intended to change, we intended to make that choice, but mentally we couldn't muster the logic or the courage to do so.

Olivia knew she should tell Noah "no!" and push him away, but she let him kiss her anyway. A few evenings later when they were together in his car, she knew she should tell him "no!" but they parked out behind the football stadium anyway. When he invited her over to his house while his parents were out of town, she knew she should tell him "no!" but she went there anyway. When they ended up in bed and he was getting aggressive, she knew she should tell him "no!" but she participated anyway. Today, some six weeks later as she prepared to sit down with her mother and tell her she was pregnant, all Olivia could think was ... How in the world did I let this happen?

A man can do what he ought to do;
and when he says he cannot, it is because he will not.

Johann Fichte, German Philosopher

As these words infer, the majority of the time we have full knowledge of the problem, difficulty, or disappointment our actions may cause, but we lack the will-power to make a better choice. We decide to have fun or enjoyment now by putting aside any thoughts about how our actions could hurt ourselves, or others. However, when the train wreck occurs, we will likely think about it, almost every day, for the remainder of our lives.

Don't continue doing something you know you shouldn't be doing, believing that a train wreck won't happen in your life. Use your choices to "switch tracks" and get on board to doing better things with your life. Use your choices to ride on to much better circumstances. You can adjust your life—or even completely change it—depending on the choices you have the will power to make.

Good choices are very powerful ... they can even prevent train wrecks in our lives.

The Choice to
End Up Somewhere

Sounds silly, doesn't it … the choice to end up somewhere. But many of us go through life doing things day after day without ever stopping to think about where we are headed. We tend to take life one day at a time and fail to make clear-cut choices about the direction of our life and what we want to accomplish with it. Then one day, we wake up and ask ourselves, How did I get here? Our intentions were to end up somewhere better, but we never took the time to define where that was. Elbert Hubbard, author of *Little Journeys to the Homes of the Great*, explained why we let this happen:

It does not take much strength to do things,
but it requires a great deal of strength to decide what to do.

We have a tendency to go along with what other people think or do. We frequently believe that the other guy knows what he is doing and just accept the influences that come our way. However, when we live this way and don't define where we want to go with our lives, we become shaped by other people's thinking and miss the opportunity to become the unique individuals we were intended to be. Lewis Carroll, writing in his classic *Alice in Wonderland*, gave us this simple, but very applicable, conversation between Alice and the Cat:

Alice: *"Would you tell me, please, which way I ought to walk from here?"*

The Cat: *"That depends a good deal on where you want to get to."*

Alice: *"I don't much care where."*

The Cat: *"Then it doesn't matter which way you walk."*

Alice: *"So long as I get somewhere."*

The Cat: *"Oh, you're sure to do that … if you only walk long enough."*

Those of us who are willing to walk through life without making difficult choices concerning our life's direction will most assuredly end up "somewhere." But it's not likely to be a place or circumstance that we will really enjoy. Here are four thoughts that will help you to make more effective choices and take your life to a very special "somewhere" one of these days.

There is a process of making a good choice.
Unless you are the luckiest person in the world, good things don't just happen. You have to be willing to think, to take the time to evaluate the alternatives, and to prioritize the options in an effective way. It may take days, weeks, or even months to make an important choice. But that's okay. Trigger-happy choice-making almost never works in real life. Defining what you want to accomplish with your life deserves extra time and thinking.

You should listen to your own drumbeat.
We all have special interests, feelings, and motivations that point to our "somewhere" in life. The challenge for you and me is to determine where these signals are telling us to go and then make the choices that will allow us to get there.

You should check the intent of your choice.
Will the choice you are about to make benefit others? Selfish choices, made only to benefit ourselves, never work out in the long run. It's only the choices that make other lives better, even in some small way, that create a special life for us.

You should be smart about the choices you make.
You may have the world's best intentions, but never accomplish any of them if you are not willing to use your head to carefully evaluate the choices you make. As one person put it:

Nature gave us two ends — one to sit on and one to think with. Success or failure is dependent on the one we use the most.

Be sure to put the correct end to work in your life. And may your "somewhere" be special indeed.

Section 11
Thinking Wisely

PERSONAL NOTES AND REMINDERS

*The
choices
we make today
will define our lives
tomorrow.*

12

DEVELOPING A MEANINGFUL LIFE

There is no better time to launch your efforts to develop a more meaningful life than now. Young or old, good or bad, clever or not, lucky or otherwise, if you need to do so, you can start now—this very day—making better and more effective choices ... choices that will allow your life to become more meaningful to you and more beneficial to those around you.

Because each of us is different, there's no one "explanation" of how to develop a more meaningful life, and this section is not intended to accomplish that objective. But achieving success and meaning in life does depend on listening to our hearts, valuing the feelings we have on the inside, and making the choices that allow us to follow where these "signals" are directing us to go.

CHOICES ADDRESSED IN THIS SECTION

The Choice to

Check with Your Heart
Value What's on the Inside
Be Mindful of What It Takes

The Choice to
Check with Your Heart

It's hard to determine which body part is the most important, but, if asked, the most common answers would likely be the *head* and the *heart*. Certainly we need all parts working well and in cooperation with each other, but these two seem to have added significance. Our vote here is for the heart because, regardless of how smart we are, life can turn out to be a disappointing experience if our heart—and the love that it supports and conveys—is not functioning well within us. Carl Jung, the founder of analytical psychology, pointed to the significance of the heart with this observation:

Your vision will become clear only when you look into your heart. Who looks outside, dreams. Who looks inside, awakens.

In spite of our hearts' significance, we seem to be more concerned about our heads. We place a high value on education, believing that the more we know, the better our life will be. We make an effort to be informed by tracking the news, weather, and world events throughout the day. And we believe that reading good books adds to our knowledge and understanding. In fact, all of these are important and necessary. But it's our hearts that impart the love and feelings that are so important in many of the choices we make. Doctors may listen to our hearts to make sure they are beating okay, but you and I need to check with them to make sure they are guiding our lives and the choices we are making.

Most of us agree it's good to stop and think about the extent to which our hearts are guiding our lives—a personal heart check, if you will. The best way to do this is to take an honest look at yourself and evaluate the real focus of your life. Our heads lead us to focus on *ourselves*, our hearts to focus on *others*. While we need some balance between the two, many of us have our dials turned almost exclusively on ourselves … a real indication that our heads, not our hearts, are steering our lives.

If this self-assessment indicates that you need more heart in your life, how do you turn yourself back in that direction? You do it by showing—in real and specific ways—your love and concern for others. Clearly, the love that emanates from our lives comes from our hearts. So, we have to show others that we care about them if we want to put more heart into our lives. Two things are important here:

Showing your love for those you know.
We tend to take the special people in our lives for granted. Whether it is our parents, our spouse, our neighbors, or our friends, we tend to think of these relationships as automatic and not in need of special attention. Just not true. Make it a point to let these special people know that you love or care deeply about them.

Showing your concern for those you don't know.
There are dozens of volunteer groups in your city or area that are working to help hundreds, maybe thousands, of people have better lives by providing food, shelter, or special assistance. If you want to really increase your heart's role in your life, get actively involved in one of these. And help people you don't know have a better life.

It's the love in our hearts—not just having it, but actually sharing it in some way—that makes life worthwhile. Love is the factor that positions us to do positive things and connects our lives to others. There may be many important loves in your life, including your work or hobby, but none is more important than the love and concern you have for other people, those you know and those you don't. As you think about putting more heart into your life, remember how Andrew Lloyd Webber characterized the effect of love in his song "Love Changes Everything":

Love ... love changes everything; hands and faces, earth and sky.
Love ... love changes everything; how you live and how you die.

Make sure your heart is playing an active role in the choices you are making. It can be an amazing guide indeed.

The Choice to
Value What's on the Inside

We tend to focus a lot on our appearance. Am I dressed right for the party? Does my hair look okay? Does this tie go with this jacket? No question, we spend an inordinate amount of time being concerned about what's on the outside in an effort to impress or be accepted by those around us.

But will all of this attention directed to our outside really help us accomplish something worthwhile with our lives? Obviously, you and I need to be clean and presentable and, when appropriate, professionally dressed. But if we place more attention on our outside than what's going on inside—in our hearts, our minds, and our souls—we are, in my opinion, living life in the wrong way. Amanda Hocking, the USA Today best-selling author of the Trylle Trilogy, explained the folly of being liked just for our looks this way:

> *Being liked for the way you look is worse*
> *than not being liked at all.*

It takes less than an hour, maybe a little longer on special occasions, to get our outside appearance in order. And if we don't like it, we can start all over tomorrow. But conditioning our heart to be concerned about others and equipping our minds with worthwhile information requires the better part of a lifetime. How you look is really no big deal. But failing to pay attention to how you are "dressed on the inside" could result in a life that is wasted. Two things to remember:

To use our hearts.
Our hearts will direct us to the most important things we do with our lives. It is the feelings in our hearts that attune us to the needs of others. It is our hearts that direct us to our intended purpose in life. It is our hearts that display the goodness within us and define the type of person we are.

It is only with the heart that one can see rightly;
what is essential is invisible to the eye.

Antoine de Saint-Exupéry, *The Little Prince*

To develop our minds.
Our minds require a significant development effort: attending school, listening to others, researching items of interest, having first-hand experiences, and on and on. Being knowledgeable is always better than living in an ill-informed way. But it takes effective choices followed by hard work to equip your mind with good and helpful information.

Biology gives you a brain. Life turns it into a mind.

Jeffrey Eugenides, *Middlesex*

Leigh Anne was focused on her looks, how she was dressed, and whether others approved of her appearance. She kept right in step with the latest fashion trends, had the requisite piercings and tattoos, and seldom passed up a chance to look in the mirror. Leigh Anne didn't worry too much about her grades in high school and she dropped out of college because it "just wasn't her thing." She spent little time actually helping others and, as a result, had few close friends. Leigh Anne is now forty and starting to wonder about things. Not that Leigh Anne has ever done anything bad or wrong, but she now wonders if she missed something in the way she had chosen to live her life. She sat there one day thinking, "Maybe just looking good hasn't been as important as I thought."

Over time, our looks will fade and become less important. But our hearts and minds can be developed, grow in significance, and become the forces that create a unique individual living a meaningful and authentic life. Don't spend too much time worrying about what's on your outside. Don't devote all of your energies to dressing up your outside life while your inside life falls in disrepair. Focusing on the inside—your heart, mind, and soul—can add special meaning to your life. It's another powerful choice that only you can make.

The Choice to
Be Mindful of What It Takes

We want to achieve meaningful and important things with our lives. When we get to the end, we want to be able to look back and feel good about the life we lived. But in spite of wanting this feeling, we tend to just accept things as they come, and spend little time thinking about what it takes to fully develop the life we're living. So, consider this important question: Are you just accepting life as it comes to you, or are you making a real effort to fully develop the life you have been given?

While each of our lives is unique and lived in our own special ways, there are three basic things we should do if we want to maximize the potential that our lives possess. These include:

Committing to an extended effort.

It takes time to develop a meaningful life. How long? Years for sure, and in some cases an entire lifetime. Whatever the work, project, or vocation you choose for your life, the development will take an extended and unceasing effort if you want to achieve a special result. Some people just aren't willing to work hard enough to make it happen. It's not a matter of being lucky or being born on the right side of the tracks. It's a matter of your devotion and commitment to achieve the more important goals you have established for your life.

Developing an exceptional level of knowledge about something.

Whether through academics, years in the marketplace, or a focused research effort, you have to develop a real understanding of what you are doing to gain those insightful perspectives that only knowledge can provide. Effort is vitally important, no question about that, but knowing what you're doing is equally so. We will never know it all, but developing an exceptional level of knowledge about something is vital. Find the one thing of greatest interest to you and become one of the world's leading experts about it.

Taking some risks.
If you are choosing to achieve something important and mean-ingful with your life, there will be times when you can't really be sure how things might work out. You may even become fearful that you will fail and your efforts won't attain the desired results. At times like these, you have to rely on your feelings inside—on your heart and your head—to provide you with some indication of what you should do. Whatever that feeling turns out to be, we are well-served to remember that sometimes we have to go with our gut and take the risk, sometimes a huge one, if we are to make our vision and the life we want to become reality.

To fly you have to begin taking risks.
If you don't want to,
maybe the best thing is just to give up,
and keep walking forever.

Jorge Bucay, Psychotherapist

There are few guarantees in life. And unless you intend to live a quiet and easy one, possibly ignoring your life's purpose and what you are being called to do, there will always be risks involved. In fact, the more you want to do or achieve, the greater those risks will be. There are many types of risks, including business risks, relationship risks, helping-others risks, improving-the-community risks, and more. The idea is not to avoid or live without risks, but to assess them and, when that all-important moment comes, to muster the courage to make the choice you need to make.

If you want to accomplish something meaningful with your life, remember to do these three things—to commit to an extended effort, to become exceptionally knowledgeable about what is of greatest interest to you, and to be willing to take risks when you face that moment of decision concerning what you want to achieve with your life. You have been given your life free of charge. It's up to you—and you alone—to determine how much you are willing to invest to make something special out of it.

Section 12
Developing a Meaningful Life

PERSONAL NOTES AND REMINDERS

The
choices
we make today
will define our lives
tomorrow.

13

MAKING YOUR LIFE
MORE ENJOYABLE

Almost without exception, we all want to enjoy our lives. We want to feel we are making progress and heading our lives in the right direction. But in spite of wanting such enjoyment from our living, we have times in our lives when we encounter disappointments or feel that we have not attained as much as we would have liked.

Yes, we have important goals and we're working to achieve them, but we have a long way to go before we get there. Yes, we want the best for those around us, but we have this family member or friend who has turned out to be a real disappointment. Yes, we've worked hard, but we haven't accomplished as much at school or in business as we had intended. No question, things happen during each of our lives that bring us great concern or even outright disappointment.

The question, of course, is this: What can we do to make our lives more enjoyable? There is no simple answer here, but there are things we can specifically do to bring more enjoyment into our lives. This section addresses four of the more important ones.

CHOICES ADDRESSED IN THIS SECTION

The Choice to

Eliminate Regrets
Feel Better about Life
Put More Joy into Your Life
Value the Progress You Made Today

The Choice to
Eliminate Regrets

Experiencing regret can make our lives anything but enjoyable. Typically, it's the result of a bad choice. We chose to do something we now wish we hadn't done ... regrets of *commission*, if you will. But regret can also come from missed opportunities, from not doing something we now wish we had made an effort to do. These, of course, are regrets of *omission*. Sydney J. Harris, the Chicago-based journalist and author, made this distinction between the two:

Regret for the things we did can be tempered by time;
it is regret for the things we didn't do that is inconsolable.

There is wisdom in his insight. We can get over our mistakes as time tends to heal things and living in a much better way helps us forget about the past. But to make up for something we didn't do—and now wish we had—is an impossible task indeed. Bronnie Ware, who spent many years as a caregiver for the dying, outlined in her book *The Top Five Regrets of the Dying* the most frequently heard regrets from her patients. Here are the ones Bronnie explained were heard most often:

1. I wish I'd lived true to myself, not the life others expected of me.

2. I wish I hadn't worked so hard.

3. I wish I'd had the courage to express my feelings.

4. I wish I had stayed in touch with my friends.

5. I wish I had let myself be happier.

Think for a moment: What have you not done that you would regret if you never have the chance to do it? What regrets of omission would be on your list? If you devote some careful thought to your answers, you will, in effect, be creating a road map to areas in your life where you need to make some important choices. Consider these five questions, reflective of Bronnie's five points, to help you decide what your answers might be:

What is your heart telling you to do?

Who do you need to reach out to in some way?

Is there a special cause you would like to be involved in?

Do you have old friends you haven't contacted in years?

Is there one thing you have intended your whole life to do?

Many of us let life slip by without taking stock of the things we wish we had done. However, it is never too late to benefit from a re-grets-of-omission exercise. You can stop and perform one right now. Here's a suggestion about how to do it. Think about your regrets and make a list of them. This may not be a long list ... in fact, it may have only one thing on it. Your entries should not include impossibilities, but rather important tasks or activities you are willing to tackle in the coming months or even years. Then, start making the choices you need to make to take action on at least one regret on your list. After completing your work on that one, check it off and, if you have more, keep going.

If only.
Those must be the two saddest words in the world.

Mercedes Lackey

Our choices are the tools we use to eliminate our regrets. Don't die with your regrets. Make the choices you need to make to elim-inate them instead, making life more enjoyable for you and others.

The Choice to
Feel Better about Life

Sometimes we feel a bit hopeless about things. Maybe we're having difficulties with someone close to us. Maybe it's our work or academic life. Or it could be the dawning realization that our life is not working out the way we had hoped. Whatever the cause, we all encounter hopeless feelings at some point in our lives. The question is, What can we do to feel better about things?

Many of us simply avoid thinking about a difficult situation, waiting and hoping for things to get better. But that seldom works. However, we can start the process of heading our life in a better direction by acknowledging that difficult times can actually work to our advantage. Not only do we learn from difficult experiences, but they also give us an opportunity to make some new choices in our lives. Difficult times can actually position us for greater achievements in the future.

There are no easy answers here, but one thing is for sure. As stated several times in this book, at no time in our lives are our choices more important than when we are feeling down or disappointed about things. We can't change the past, but we can certainly change the future. We have to work our way out of such circumstances and our choices allow us to do exactly that. Here are two of the most important choices you can make to help the way you feel and give you some objectives for the future.

Do something helpful for someone.

When times are tough, we almost always focus on ourselves. Interestingly, that's the opposite of what we should do. The key is not to focus exclusively on yourself, but to do something that will make another person's life better. It doesn't have to be something major … an email or phone call, a personal visit to see how someone is doing, or possibly helping someone over a financial hump if you are able to do so. It's amazing how reaching out and helping another person can change our lives and in a significant way. This Hindu proverb says it rather well:

Help thy brother's boat across,
and lo thine own has reached the shore!

Focus on your life's intended purpose.
You are here for a reason. There is something you are intended to do with your life. During difficult times like these, we should redouble our efforts to determine what that purpose is—what our interests, our hearts, and the needs of others are saying to us. By thinking about and, in effect, decoding these influences, we gain insight into our real purpose in life. Our work to confirm and live out our purpose in life not only reenergizes us, but it also gets our lives refocused on what's really important.

There is no greater gift you can give or receive than
to honor your calling. It's why you were born.
And how you become most truly alive.

Oprah Winfrey

Obviously, the few words written here can't totally change your life. That will require work and effort on your part. But with the right choices, you can start a journey to a better place. If you're willing to start doing helpful things for others and to work to confirm the intended purpose of your life, you can head your life in a better—and much more enjoyable—direction. In fact, that journey could start this very day.

I shouldn't describe choices as miracles, but they come close to being exactly that, especially when life is difficult for us. Circumstances are not likely to change on their own until we start making the choices that will change them. Change your choices and change your life. We know it's not quite that simple, but clearly better choices create better circumstances and, at some point, a better and more enjoyable life as well.

The Choice to
Put More Joy Into Your Life

Life itself can't bring you joy,
unless you really will it.
Life just gives you time and space,
it's up to you to fill it.

This little poem, which has been around for many years, makes a big point: Our life provides us with many opportunities, but what we do with them is determined by the choices we make … *unless you really will it*, as the poem says. Therefore, it's not the life we have been given that counts, but how we choose to live it that determines the level of enjoyment we receive.

As just a few minor examples, we can …

… show respect for other people, or just be indifferent toward their circumstances.

… work hard to accomplish something important, or be lazy and let things slide.

… accept others as they are, or take those verbal shots that never improve anything.

… be the first one to apologize, or stay angry and "out of sorts" for the rest of our lives.

We have choices. How we use them is up to us.

When it comes to enjoying life, we typically think if we had more we'd be happier—more money, more house, more car, more sense, more luck, and on and on we go. But having more joy in our lives is not about *getting* more. It's almost totally dependent on *giving* more. It's important to understand that joy doesn't come from getting things for ourselves, but from what we give to others. John

Bunyan, in his book *The Pilgrim's Progress*, gave us this short but insightful explanation that applies to how giving works:

A man there was, tho' some did count him mad;
the more he gave, the more he had.

If your life lacks a certain amount of joy, make a choice to …

… *give* your concern to someone by calling to say you were thinking about them,

… *give* your caring to an elderly friend by visiting to see how she is doing,

… *give* your time to volunteer at the nonprofit fundraiser, or to deliver meals to shut-ins,

… *give* your energy to rebuild a family's house that was damaged in a storm, or

… *give* your financial support to a friend you know is having a tough time.

Granted, it can be difficult to change our focus from putting ourselves first to being more concerned about those around us. It doesn't seem to be the natural thing to do. But it works. The more you sincerely do for others, the happier you will be … no question about it. B. C. Forbes, founder of *Forbes* magazine, explained this phenomenon about life in this way:

The human being who lives only for himself finally reaps nothing but unhappiness. Selfishness corrodes. Unselfishness ennobles, and satisfies. Don't put off the joy derivable from doing helpful, kindly things for others.

Whatever you choose to give, joy will come when you focus your life on the needs of others. Making life more enjoyable … it's all about giving. Getting has almost nothing to do with it.

The Choice to
Value The Progress You Made Today

Most of us set out in life to achieve something important. We believe that attaining an important goal will make us happy and hopefully it will. Whether it's a personal goal, a career goal, or a family goal, we tend to focus on the goal and achieving the end result. In doing so, we frequently think about how much further we have to go to achieve our objective.

Our thoughts tend to be something like these:

When I become a VP, I'll feel like I've accomplished something.

When I lose twenty pounds, I'll feel so much better.

When we save enough to buy that house, I'll be so relieved.

No question, accomplishing an important goal can create a great sense of satisfaction within us. In addition, we tend to achieve more when we establish important, longer-term objectives for ourselves. But we can spend so much time thinking about the ultimate goal that we completely overlook the satisfaction that can come from the progress we made today. Satisfaction from doing good work at the office *today*. From losing a few ounces of weight *today*. From foregoing a purchase and saving a little money *today*. If we stop and think about it, we can derive a great deal of satisfaction from the small amount of progress we make each day.

A little progress each day
adds up to big results.

An Important Thought

Happiness can come from our little achievements, not just our big ones. We can be happy that we made today count by taking one step toward our goal ... by doing good work, by completing our exercise routine, by saving some money, or by improving someone else's life in some small way. John Wooden, the basketball coach at UCLA who won ten national championships, reminded us of the importance of doing the little things well:

Little things make big things happen.

Important, long-range goals energize us and motivate us as we go through our day. We need these goals to guide our choices and provide a frame of reference for our lives. But the small amount of progress you make today is extremely important as well. Most big goals are accomplished through a series of small steps, so moving one step closer today is no small matter.

After his last checkup, Landon decided that he needed to lose 110 pounds, going from 310 to an even 200. He had been thinking about it for years, but he finally made a firm choice to do so. At the suggestion of a friend, he made a poster board above his scale and entered his weight every morning when he got up. As he looked at the chart this morning, he saw that he had lost thirty-seven pounds over the past five months. He was still seventy-three pounds away from his objective, but, oh my, did he feel good about seeing the progress he had made. He looked forward to more of those feelings in the days ahead.

While you're on your way to a big accomplishment in your life, take the time to enjoy the progress, small though it may be, you made today. Working hard today merits a feeling of accomplishment as you drive home tonight. Solid exercise time today can provide you with a feeling of satisfaction shortly after you finish your workout. And saving some money for a house today can give you a real sense of pride as you go to sleep tonight. Today's progress is very important in the grand scheme of things, and you should take the time to feel good about it—and truly enjoy it—as you wrap up your day.

The big celebrations will come, but by all means, have a small celebration today. Today was very important ... choosing to use it well should make you very happy.

Section 13
Making Your Life More Enjoyable

PERSONAL NOTES AND REMINDERS

*The
choices
we make today
will define our lives
tomorrow.*

14

LOOKING TO THE FUTURE

The previous section pointed out that what we do today is very important. It stressed we should value and enjoy the progress we make each day, small though it may be. Coupled with that, we also need to think about our longer-range future and where we are headed with our lives. This section, appropriately included at the end of the book, is intended to help you think about the choices that will have long-term implications for your life.

CHOICES ADDRESSED IN THIS SECTION

The Choice to

Focus on the Future, Not the Past

Overcome Your Fear

Recognize How Important You Can Be

Set High Expectations

Give Your Life Some Careful Thought

Be Well Remembered

Live in the Goodness

The Choice to
Focus on the Future, Not the Past

We all have things in our past that we would like to go back and change. But changing history is not an option. And since we can't change the past, we should focus on the changes and choices we can make in the future. We should work on the life we want to have in the months and years ahead and not worry about the life we've already lived ... the one that is now in the history book. While there are many choices we can make to develop a more meaningful life, two seem to be fundamentally important:

Becoming a kind and giving person.
I don't care how much you know, how much money you have, or how cute or good-looking you are, you are almost certain not to achieve your purpose in life if you aren't kind and giving to those around you. Life works much better for people who are genuinely nice to others, but almost never for those who are unkind or thoughtless. Being kind and giving are the most important factors in determining how we make others feel. The world likes nice people; the opposite type, not so much. That's just the way it is. There is no substitute for being kind and giving to others.

The simplest acts of kindness are by far more powerful than a thousand heads bowing in prayer.

Mahatma Gandhi

Becoming who you are intended to be.
As mentioned several times in this book, you are here for a reason. Your life has an intended purpose. You already have certain clues to this purpose, including your interests, your motivations, and the needs of those around you. It is up to you to decide what, collectively, these signals are saying to you. It's an exciting feeling to know that your life has been given to you so that you can use it to help

others and help make the world a better place. There is a purpose for your life … one intended specifically for you … the challenge is to confirm it and then live to fulfill it.

> *You were put on this earth to achieve your greatest self,*
> *to live out your purpose, and to do it courageously.*
>
> Steve Maraboli, *Life, the Truth, and Being Free*

Daniel was a first-class jerk, that's the only way to put it. He had been spoiled growing up, was very selfish, and never thought too much about helping others. All he thought about was money. He lived to support a lavish lifestyle and, as you might guess, did very little to improve the town where he lived. Today, he has a big house, three cars, lots of toys, but few real friends.

Hannah was a sweet girl and always quick to help her schoolmates. She volunteered to visit at the nursing home every week and remained active in her church. She worked her way through college, made good grades, and wanted to be a successful mom someday. She married "my best friend" as she called him shortly after graduation. Today, she doesn't have a lot of money, but she has a wonderful family, a meaningful career as a home-schooling mom, and lots of close friends.

Which of these two lives would you chose to have?

As we look to the future, it's important to remember that we are not here to get things for ourselves (like Daniel), but to help those around us have better and more enjoyable lives (as Hannah was doing). For those of us who come to understand this, life takes on a special meaning.

Make your future count … be kind to those around you, and work to determine what you have been put on this earth to do. May you and I recognize the importance of these two things as we work to build a life that is meaningful and worthwhile.

The Choice to
Overcome Your Fear

The easy choices come and go with little thought or emotion. However, our more life-defining choices can give us pause, even create fear within us. Making a career change, standing up for a cause we believe in, or doing that one big thing we've always wanted to do can create fear within us. Such fear can slow us down, cause us to make safer choices, or, in some instances, to make no choice at all.

As you think about your future, it's important to note that fear can impact us in both *negative* and *positive* ways. It's negative when fear keeps us from doing something special with our lives. On the other hand, "running scared" can be a positive condition if it causes us to work harder than we ever have, to pay more attention to the details, and to listen more intently to those around us. Our reactions to fear can, in fact, be important ingredients in achieving success.

When we are considering a life-changing choice, it is wise to do our homework. Being equipped with a certain level of understanding is always beneficial. However, our feelings about the choice can be very important as well. Do we feel this is something we were meant to do? Do we feel this choice is in concert with the intended purpose of our life? While logic can be helpful during such life-defining moments, our feelings about what we're going to do can be even more so. Spanish philosopher George Santayana reminded us of the importance of these feelings with this observation:

Columbus found a whole new world,
but had no chart, save one that faith deciphered in the skies.

Life can be routine at times. In fact, we can become so comfortable that we let something that we always wanted to do float to the back of our mind, maybe even out of our thoughts altogether. But we have to remember that we are here for a reason and that we come pre-equipped with certain qualities that, over time, point us to it. We have to listen to our interests, our motivations, and how we are impacted by the needs of others to determine our purpose in life. You most likely have felt something pushing your life in a certain direction. The challenge is not only to identify what that "push" is telling us to do but also to muster the courage to do it. The Bible in Deuteronomy 30:11-14 emphasizes the importance of listening to your life and what it is telling you to do with these words:

> *This command I am giving you today is not too difficult for you to understand or perform. It is not up in heaven, so distant that you must ask, "Who will go to heaven and bring it down so we can hear and obey it?" It is not beyond the sea, so far away that you must ask, "Who will cross the sea to bring it to us?" ... the message is very close at hand; it is on your lips and in your heart.*

If you're going to do something special with your life, you must not let fear hold you back. Reach inside and call on yourself to make that all-important choice, even in the face of those fearful feelings. In other words, there will be times in your life when you simply have to suck it up and go for it. In those moments, rely on the desires of your heart to support the choice you feel you should make.

Fear is a powerful enemy
but not one too strong to overcome.

Kiley Kellermeyer, *Damselle in Distress*

Don't let fear keep you from doing something special with your life. After all, that's what you're here for. You are prewired with an intended purpose, but it will take insight, courage, and some good choices to achieve it. Rely on your heart to chart your course and your choices to move you along your intended way. You're a very special person ... don't let fear keep your life from being special as well.

The Choice to
Recognize How Important You Can Be

We tend to see ourselves as average, and don't often stop to consider how important we can really be. "I'm just an everyday person," you say. "There's nothing that significant about me." Well, you may be totally wrong about that.

We come in contact with many people during a typical day ... ordinary, everyday people for sure. But over the years, I've come to appreciate just how important being one of these everyday people really is. Wonderful people who greet us at church, nice neighbors who help us in special ways, associates at work who encourage us each day, the nice ladies who wait on people at the cleaners, those ... well, you get the point. It's everyday people who make such a difference in our lives—who greet us, help us, and make us feel special in so many ways.

Many times we don't recognize the importance of our role as one of these everyday people. We are typically more concerned about our own lives than about how important we can be in the lives of others. Yes, there are "special people" such as movie stars and professional athletes, but it's those very important everyday people who really make our lives enjoyable and worthwhile. As we go about our roles as one of these very important everyday people, here are three things to keep in mind:

It's all about how we make others feel ...
There are no secrets here. Our importance to others depends almost solely on how we make them feel. Such feelings can develop from chance encounters, from time spent with family members, from special occasions with friends or business associates, and even from our interactions with store personnel as we run our errands each day. Every contact we have with someone, however insignificant it may seem, provides us with an opportunity to make someone feel special, to show we care about them, and appreciate what they

do for us. Barbara De Angelis, author of *How to Make Love All the Time*, explained it this way:

Love and kindness are never wasted.
They always make a difference.
They bless the one who receives them,
and they bless you, the giver.

Our lives are transformed from ordinary to extraordinary by what we do for others ...
You can be so important to others if you will reach out and touch their lives in your own special way. It may be as simple as offering a nice smile or a word of encouragement to someone. It may be buying a cartload of groceries and delivering them to a family in need. It may be volunteering to help with a special project in your community. It could be one of hundreds of ways you could make a difference in someone's life. Yes, it takes extra effort to do these things, but the impact of those efforts can make a major difference in the lives of others and in your life as well.

Somewhere along the way, we must learn
that there is nothing greater than to do something for others.

Dr. Martin Luther King, Jr.

You can be as important as you choose to be ...
It may sound silly right now, but it's true ... you can become one of the most important people in the world to someone around you. It depends on your choices and how you make them feel. When someone knows you truly care about them, your importance in their life increases significantly. And creating such feelings is not a once-in-a-lifetime opportunity. It's an opportunity we have many times throughout each day.

You and I may not be movie stars or professional athletes. But we can be one of these so very important everyday people. And what would the world be without people like that?

The Choice to
Set High Expectations

When I was young, my mother gave me this advice: "Michael, you need to have something important to look forward to." When I got older, I understood what she meant … that our expectations play a very important role in the way we live our lives.

Granted, we look forward to nice dinners or weekends away. Such expectations are nice to think about. But what about the expectations we have for our lives? What do we expect to accomplish? What type of person do we expect to be? And how do we expect to use our life to help others? These are important questions, and answering each of them helps us set expectations for our lives.

But setting high expectations can be dangerous business. It increases the chances of disappointment when things don't work out the way we planned. In fact, for that very reason many people prefer to take life one day at a time, be spontaneous, and not expect too much from themselves. They will have fewer disappointments living that way. True, but not setting real expectations for our lives and working to make them a reality can bring great disappointments too … often when it's too late in life to do anything about it.

Not failure, but low aim, is a crime.

Ernest Holmes, Author of *The Science of Mind*

Setting high expectations helps us in a number of ways:

Helps us to make more productive choices each day.
Our expectations provide a way for us to gauge a choice we are about to make. Will this choice help me achieve my objective, or not? Generally, the higher our expectations, the more meaningful our choices will be. The self-fulfilling aspect of the well-known saying that "things usually turn out the way we expect them to" comes from the influence that our expectations have on the choices we make.

Directs us toward our intended purpose in life.
If you believe, as I do, that your life has a unique purpose, then you know the intentions for your life are significant. You have been pre-equipped to do something special with your life. Setting well-thought-out expectations puts your life on a path for doing these good and important things. It is through those expectations and the choices we make to fulfill them that we ultimately achieve our intended purpose in life. Josiah Gilbert Holland, the American novelist, poet, and editor, expressed it this way:

> God puts special instruments into every man's hands
> by which to make himself and achieve his mission.

Positions us to do meaningful things.
There are significant problems in this country and throughout the world that need attention and, ultimately, to be resolved. These aren't simple matters and aren't easy to fix. We need people with high expectations to raise their hands ("Send me!"), address these difficult situations, and work to make life better for those involved. Don't underestimate your personal potential for making a big difference in the lives of others and in this world. Rev. Edwin Chapin, an early editor of the *Christian Leader*, gave us this view of the importance of individuals:

> Not armies, not nations, have advanced the race;
> but here and there, in the course of the ages,
> an individual has stood up and cast his shadow over the world.

So set high expectations ... to be a good person, to help the people around you, and to accomplish something special with your life. Regardless of your situation or circumstances at this very moment, you can achieve significant things with the life you have been given. It comes down to the choices you are willing to make. Most of our choices are routine, but now and then life calls us to make big and important choices and to set some very high expectations. Maybe that time for you is now.

The Choice to
Give Your Life Some
Careful Thought

Jimmy Williams had been a pretty good athlete in high school. After he graduated, he started working at small garment manufacturer and hanging out most evenings with his buddies. He never thought about doing much else. He went on to several jobs in small manufacturing companies around town. But, by the age of forty-six, Jimmy had witnessed each of these manufacturers close down as their production was moved to other countries. This left Jimmy without many options. His circumstances forced him stop and think about his life and what he might do now. As he did, he reflected on how he had always simply gone along with things, and never made an attempt to do something original or start the home rehab business he wrote about in his senior paper. He sat there this fall afternoon wondering what might have happened if he had thought more about his life and what he wanted to do.

We don't always stop and think carefully about what we're doing or a choice we are about to make. In fact, much of our personal wisdom comes from mistakes we made when we failed to give much thought to what we were saying or doing. Therefore, it's important for us to recognize the connection between the effectiveness of our *thinking* and the effectiveness of our *lives*. To improve our lives, we must improve our thinking. As this insight by Albert Einstein points out, we need to become better thinkers as we go through life:

> *We cannot solve our problems with the same thinking we used when we created them.*

And the need for better thinking has never been greater. The world is more complicated. Conflicts between nations are at all-time highs. Politicians refuse to work together for the good of all. Crime and violence in our cities has increased concerns about individual safety. Schools are turning out less-than-well-informed students.

Social media is influencing us in not-so-good ways. Long-standing personal values are no longer important. The evidence of poor thinking is all around us.

To be able to stand in the midst of this fray and make independent and well-informed choices, you must be a good and effective thinker. Therefore, you must honestly evaluate your ability to think though a situation to determine what is best for you. If you are deficient in your ability to think, start taking more time and doing more homework before you make your choice.

Careful thinking is our most important choice-making tool. Quick decisions are vastly overrated and are typically the ones that cause us trouble. To get the most out of your life experience, you will always be in a better position to make your choice if you take the time you need to think things over. Ed Burger, author of *The 5 Elements of Effective Thinking*, explained it this way:

Remember: Extraordinary people are just ordinary people who are thinking differently.

Back to Jimmy ... he spent most of that fall month, now twenty years ago, thinking about his life and what he wanted to do with it. He not only talked to his close friend who worked at the bank, but he also looked up his old high school shop teacher, Mr. Plunkett, and sought his advice. He got online and did some research about the home rehab business and how he might fit into it. After these discussions and the online reading he had done, Jimmy thought carefully about what he might do with his life. He then made the choice to start his own home rehab business. It had been tough at first, but his friend at the bank helped him through some of those tough spots and Jimmy put in very long hours working on his projects each day. He not only became a successful home rehabber, but went on from there to start building new homes. Now, at the age of sixty-six, he owns the largest home construction company in town.

Make sure you stop and give your life some careful thought. It's an important choice to make.

The Choice to
Be Well Remembered

My friend Ed had the knack of making everyone feel like they were his very best friend. Whenever I was around Ed, I felt important and that I mattered to him. Cancer took Ed from us almost thirty years ago, but hardly a week goes by that I don't think about him and how great he made us feel.

What will people think or say about you after you are dead and gone? Will they remember you as someone who was helpful to others or selfish and self-absorbed? Will they remember you as someone who knew what you were talking about or one who always seemed to be short on the facts? Will they remember how you worked to achieve something special with your life or as one who wasted a lot of the opportunities you had? If you died today, how would you be remembered?

This is not a subject most of us want to stop and think about. We would much prefer to focus on the here and now and what we will be doing in the coming days, especially the fun and enjoyable things. It's no fun to think about being dead. Nevertheless, taking the time to think about how you will be remembered can be very helpful if you are honest with yourself about it. Such reflections typically point out a few areas we need to tune up to enhance the chances that we will be well remembered.

During your funeral, people will reflect on a number of things, including what you accomplished … did you do something worthwhile with your life? They'll reflect on you and your family … did you look out for and take care of the other members of your family? And they will likely reflect on you as a citizen in the community … did you do things to make life better for others? They will weigh you in many ways: Were you good or bad, giving or taking, concerned or indifferent, hardworking or lazy, and on and on. Because each of us is different, memories of us will vary greatly. However, there seems to be one thing that people will always remember about you and me. Steve Goodier, author of *A Life that Makes a Difference,* pointed us to it:

After you are gone, people may forget most of what you have said and done. But they will remember that you loved them.

Rephrasing this very appropriate quote … *they will remember how you made them feel.* And the better you made them feel as a person, the longer you will be remembered and missed. Fame and fortune seem to have a limited shelf life, but the good feelings we instill in others while we are here seem to last and provide important memories long after we are gone.

Most of us want to go to heaven, or somewhere like it, when we die. But have you ever wondered where heaven really is? Typically, we look toward the skies and think of heaven as being up there somewhere. But let's think about this. Maybe heaven, or a portion of it, is right here with us, right here on Earth. Maybe heaven includes the positive and good memories that we have of someone, and that others will have of you someday. If such is the case, I have no doubt that my friend Ed is in heaven and will always be there.

To live in hearts we leave behind is not to die.

Thomas Campbell, *Hallowed Ground*

So here we are back to our choices once again. Whether we will be well remembered depends on the choices we make while we are living, especially how we choose to treat other people and how we make them feel. If you want to live forever, as my friend Ed seems to be doing, you'll have to treat others in a special way, and show them you truly care about them.

Is the result of such good choices a ticket to heaven?

It very well could be … and in the first-class section.

The Choice to
Live in the Goodness

Our choice making is underpinned by the kind of person we want to be. A *good* person and a *bad* one are the two extremes. Most of us, of course, want to be good. But living a good life is no easy task and even with the desire to be kind and productive, we don't always conduct ourselves as we should. It would be helpful if we had something built into us that could motivate and direct us to do good things as we work to become a better person each day.

Many of us turn to organized religious groups to obtain such guidance. It helps us live a better life when we associate with other people who are trying to do the same. Others, while not religiously active in an organized way, learned from their parents or have gained important insights along the way that guide them in living in a helpful and beneficial way. But even with these positive influences, you and I can still benefit from an internal sense of direction … an everyday feeling that a successful life is less about what we do for ourselves and almost everything about what we do for others.

While writing this book, I started thinking about all the goodness in the world today. In spite of the abundance of bad choices we see, there are millions of people who, regardless of beliefs, backgrounds, or circumstances, reach out to help someone each day. So I asked myself: *What is the motivating feeling within this diverse group of individuals that creates this desire to help others?*

You can do a lot of research on this question and not arrive at a clear-cut answer. Religious beliefs, insights from others, and actual life experiences can all contribute to the answer in some way. But with no single source to provide it, at some point you and I have to answer this question for ourselves.

I decided to answer this question (for myself) and do so in this book. I share this explanation with you not to say I fully understand things, but in hopes of helping you clarify your thinking and your beliefs as well. My only strong indicator in arriving at my conclusion is what I feel inside. It's the very same feeling that has guided me in writing this book. Here are two things I've come to believe:

There is some goodness in almost everyone.
Granted, no one can explain how God works in the world. We can, however, look for actual evidence and combine it with feelings in our hearts to develop our own understanding of goodness and how it works within us. I go back to those millions of good deeds that people do for others all around the world each day. To me, these actions are living evidence of the goodness in people. And it is my belief that this goodness is God's spirit, the spirit of goodness if you will, working in and through people ... to perform miracles ... the world over ... every day.

Our choices control the level of goodness in our lives.
This brings us back to the opening point in this book, that our choices are deceivingly powerful and actually control our lives. If we pay attention to the spirit of goodness within us, we feel more in tune with choices that help others in some way. On the other hand, we can use our choices, as many people do, to totally shut out the spirit of goodness within us. You only have to read the horrible things on the news today to know this is true.

So, to live in the goodness, it seems to me, is to live under the influence of God's spirit as it works in the world through people like you and me. It's to understand we are not here for ourselves, but rather to reach out and help others have better and more meaningful lives. It's to make choices and do things that make the world a better place ... for everyone.

Be the reason someone smiles.
Be the reason someone feels loved.
Be the reason someone believes
in the goodness in people.

Roy T. Bennett, *The Light in the Heart*

Let the spirit of goodness guide you. It could be the most important choice you will ever make.

Section 14
Looking to the Future

PERSONAL NOTES AND REMINDERS

*The
choices
we make today
will define our lives
tomorrow.*

In Closing, Please Remember …

Thank you for taking the time to read this book. *Living by Choice* was intended to help people stop and think about their lives, how their choices are defining the person they are today, and how their choices can be used to shape their lives in the future. I hope it has accomplished those objectives for you.

While you and I can't control everything in our lives, we should remain mindful of the power our choices contain. They can lead us into very bad times, or they can lift our lives and help us accomplish good and important things. So, as you go on your way, please remember …

… you are the leader of your life. Good life leadership depends on being totally honest, standing up for what is good, and committing to being better and doing better in the future.

… significant accomplishments require significant efforts. Our choices aim our lives in specific directions, but must be supported by significant efforts to become reality.

… regardless of group designations, people are individuals. Almost all the individuals around us have desires and dreams just like you and me … to have happy, meaningful, and productive lives.

… exhibiting kindness is something we can always do. Whether we like or agree with another individual or not, we can always be respectful and show kindness to those we encounter each day.

… your life has a purpose and you came equipped to fulfill it. Our interests, motivations, and the needs of others are signals that, if carefully considered, will, at some point, reveal our purpose to us.

… to set high expectations for your life. Setting high expectations for our lives not only helps us make more effective day-to-day choices, but also positions us to achieve our ultimate potential.

... *to forgive others.* We all make mistakes and therefore, forgiveness is not only something we need in our lives, but it is a condition we must be willing to give to others as well.

... *talking is much easier and much less effective than doing.* While you have a right to your opinion, little will change until you roll up your sleeves and go to work to make things better.

... *to let love guide your life.* Love will guide our lives in absolutely wonderful ways if we are willing to listen for its direction and make the choices that allow us to follow where it leads.

... *to stop and think about your life.* A well-lived life requires some careful thought, some conscious choices, and a willingness to work your tail off to make it all worthwhile.

... *we are here for each other.* Our lives have not been given to us for our sole enjoyment, but to use, however we can, to help others have better and more enjoyable lives as well.

... *you are who you choose to be.* It's your choices that define the type of person you are and the kind of life you will live. We are, in fact, the person we choose to be.

Living by choice ... it's what we do, whether we realize it or not. Not only have your choices defined the life you live today, but they are available to you to adjust or outright change your life in the future. Recognizing that *we are the person we choose to be* helps you and me place a higher value on the choices we make each day. All the best to you as you work to make better choices in your life.

The Anatomy of a Choice

We can be sincere in our efforts to make an important choice, but fall short if we don't make it in a well-thought-out way. People are different, choices are different, and circumstances are different … so there is no cookie-cutter way to make an effective choice. However, here is a framework that you may find helpful as you consider the steps you should follow in making an important choice in your life:

1. Assess your situation.
Don't just assume you have a clear picture of things. Start your choice-making process by defining the current circumstances and specifically why a new or better choice is needed.

2. Confirm your alternatives (choices).
What are your options? Take some time to define the alternatives you have. Most likely, there are several choices you could make. What are they, and how would you define each one?

3. Evaluate and rank the choices you have.
There are pluses and minuses to most of the choices we can make. Here, I am suggesting that you consider what those might be and rank your alternatives—top to bottom—in some way.

4. Select the choice you need or want to make.
Select the choice you deem to be your best alternative in the current circumstances. Consider it carefully and start to think what you will have to do to fully implement it.

5. Discuss your choice with others and research as needed.
Once you have selected the choice you intend to make, work on it. Discuss your choice with people you respect, trust, and whose opinion you value. Do more research as needed.

6. Reconfirm the choice you want to make.
You may have mentally made the choice some time ago, but given the discussions you've had and any research you may have done, you need to reconfirm the choice you are about to make.

7. Make and share the choice you have made.
You need to not only personally make the choice, but also to communicate your decision to those who have helped you or been involved in the choice you have made in some way.

8. Complete your implementation plans.
Most important choices require some period of time to implement. Although you have been working on them, now is the time to activate your plans to implement the choice you made.

9. Track your progress.
In addition to tracking your progress personally, share the steps you have completed and your progress with others, including individuals you talked with when first evaluating the choice.

10. Adjust as needed, and work to complete.
Some adjustments will likely be needed as you work to complete the implementation of your choice. Stay alert to such needs and be willing to tweak your plans as needed.

11. Congratulate yourself.
Although it might be a journey you'll be on for the remainder of your life, at some point you will have activated your choice. Be sure to congratulate yourself on the change you have made.

Choice Perspectives

It is our choices, Harry, that show what we truly are,
far more than our abilities.

J.K. Rowling, *Harry Potter and the Chamber of Secrets*

~

I'll never know, and neither will you of the life you don't choose.
It was the ghost ship that didn't carry us.
There's nothing to do but salute it from the shore.

Cheryl Strayed, *Tiny Beautiful Things: Advice on Love and Life*

~

"You are fettered," said Scrooge, "Tell me why?"
"I wear the chain I forged in life," replied the Ghost.
"I made it link by link, and yard by yard; I girded it on of
my own free will, and of my own free will I wore it."

Charles Dickens, *A Christmas Carol*

~

The choices you make now, the people
you surround yourself with, they all have the potential
to affect your life, even who you are, forever.

Sarah Dessen, *The Truth about Forever*

It isn't how much you do that counts, but how
much you do well, and how often you decide right.

William Feather, American Publisher

∿

Heroes are made by the paths they choose,
not the powers they are graced with.

Brodi Ashton, *Everneath*

∿

People pay for what they do, and, still more,
for what they have allowed themselves to become.
And they pay for it very simply; by the lives they lead.

James Baldwin, *No Name in the Street*

∿

There are two primary choices in life:
to accept conditions as they exist,
or accept the responsibility for changing them.

Denis Waitley, *The Psychology of Winning*

∿

O God ... grant us in all our doubts and uncertainties,
the grace to ask what you would have us to do;
that the Spirit of wisdom may save us from all false choices.

The Book of Common Prayer

The Choices
Alphabetical Locator

64. *The Choice to* **Respect Our Differences** 138
Showing respect for others is a choice ... a choice that can significantly increase the opportunities we have to grow and learn as individuals.

65. *The Choice to* **See Others as Individuals**. 140
We tend to place people in groups ... ethnic, religious, political, and others ... and think that the people in that group are all alike. It's a very bad choice to think this way.

66. *The Choice to* **Set High Expectations**. 210
Things usually work out the way we expect them to. Therefore, setting high expectations helps us make better and more meaningful choices as we go about our lives each day.

67. *The Choice to* **Speak and Write Effectively** 112
Regardless of the advances in technology, speaking and writing remain the fundamental ways to communicate. It just makes good sense to be skillful and effective in both.

68. *The Choice to* **Stop and Think**. 160
It's almost a universal truth that poor choices are made with little or inadequate thought. If we want to make more meaningful choices, we must be willing to stop and think before we do.

69. *The Choice to* **Stop Criticizing Others** 166
Most of the criticism we provide about others is not deserved. Even when it is, we should keep our criticism to ourselves. We should get our own house in order and before criticizing others.

70. *The Choice to* **Stop Making Excuses** 164
One of the major differences between those who effectively develop their lives and those who don't is a willingness to stop making excuses and to accept responsibility for results.

71. *The Choice to* **Take Care of Your Body**. 170
Over 65 percent of Americans are either overweight or obese. Most often, it's because we are making poor choices concerning what we eat and the extent to which we exercise each day.

We "water" people's lives in many ways ... sometimes with a smile, sometimes with a kind word, sometimes with a check. Make sure you take your watering can wherever you go.

Sometimes life just doesn't work. Maybe it was something out of our control, or maybe we "dug the hole" ourselves. At no time are our choices more important than at times like these.

With so many different backgrounds, beliefs, and political preferences in our communities, how will we ever be able to work together for the good of all? We do it through respect.

My Thanks To Others

It has taken over a year to write this book. During the process, I had the help of some wonderful and very talented individuals. I would like to say a special thank you to them here.

Lindsay Jones, a very capable newspaper editor and contributor to the writings on our nonprofit website, wrestled with some of the earlier versions of the book and shaped them in her own special way. Kristen Hamilton, a very busy and capable book editor, performed an early review and provided many helpful suggestions about the book. Ginny Glass read the manuscript and provided a special written report with her suggestions.

As the book was taking shape, Brian Mauldin, retired attorney; Joe Humphries, recent college graduate; and Chris Tepedino, an aspiring writer, read the manuscript and provided some very insightful feedback. They were extremely helpful in providing edits and suggestions that further improved the book.

Christina Roth, one very professional and detailed book editor, did the final edit work and put her touches on the book … a special thanks to her not only for the edits she provided but also for her sincere interest in making the book helpful and meaningful to its readers.

About the Author
Michael L. Nelson

Michael and his wife Betty were high school sweethearts, and are graduates of the University of Mississippi. They have two grown children, both with MBAs and very successful in their own right, and three wonderful grandchildren. They are active members of Idlewild Presbyterian Church in Memphis, Tennessee.

Michael started his business career with IBM. He went on from there to become a partner in a technology equipment leasing organization, and then served as President of a technology consulting firm in Chicago. In addition, he served on the board of a Mid-south banking organization for ten years.

After selling his business interest in Chicago, Michael and Betty returned to Memphis and, shortly after, he wrote his first book, *Good Choices Good Life*. He then helped start a small educational nonprofit, which promotes good choice-making through topics on its website, www.GoodChoicesGoodLife.org.

∽

Please feel free to email any comments you may have to:
mnelson234@gmail.com

Made in the USA
Lexington, KY
15 March 2018